A Different Kind of Love

A Different Kind of Love

MICHAEL BORICH

Holt, Rinehart and Winston
New York

22031

Copyright © 1985 by Michael Borich
All rights reserved, including the right to reproduce this
book or portions thereof in any form.
Published by Holt, Rinehart and Winston,
383 Madison Avenue, New York, New York 10017.
Published simultaneously in Canada by Holt, Rinehart and
Winston of Canada, Limited.

Library of Congress Cataloging in Publication Data
Borich, Michael, 1949–
A different kind of love.
Summary: A fourteen-year-old's life with her single
mother is complicated when an overly affectionate uncle
comes to visit and she must deal with her feelings of
guilt and enjoyment.
[1. Single-parent family—Fiction.   2. Uncles—
Fiction]   I. Title.
PZ7.B648453Di   1985   [Fic]   84-22492
ISBN: 0-03-003249-0

FIRST EDITION

Design by Kate Nichols
Printed in the United States of America
10 9 8 7 6 5 4 3 2 1

ISBN 0-03-003249-0

For my sisters: *Melissa*
Linda
Laurene
Luanne

And for: *Stephanie and Lynn*

A Different Kind of Love

One

We couldn't decide what to steal.

"Just go to the back once more; the lady at the register must think we're weird or something," Jennifer whispered. We followed her down the aisle, past school supplies, and then into the cosmetic department. Jennifer bent over the mascaras as if she were deciphering hieroglyphics.

Robyn, my best friend, puckered up her face and flashed a look that said, What are we doing here? There was mild panic in her brown eyes. Usually her eyes reminded me of a cocker spaniel about to cry. Right now they opened wide and flitted past my shoulder.

"I think we'll wait outside," I said to Jennifer.

She stood up and glared at me. Then she sighed and glanced down at the package of eyeliner in her hand, measuring it as she turned it over. I expected her to thrust it in between her jeans and T-shirt—as she had shown us on the way home from school. But instead she sighed again, impatient, and bit at her lower lip.

"Yeah, me too," Robyn said. "I changed my mind about needing anything today."

"What is with you two?" Jennifer said, her teeth clenched.

"We'll wait outside, okay?" I realized I was asking permission for something I should have just done. But I didn't move.

"Forget it," Jennifer said. "Do what I—" She broke off as the lady from the cash register began a slow amble back toward us to straighten some cards in a revolving rack and replace a fallen envelope. Jennifer turned back to the makeup.

"Help you find anything, girls?" the woman asked. Her gaze bounced from me to Robyn and back to me again. She waited for one of us to speak, as if she had all the time in the world. I shook my head and looked at Robyn.

She managed a grin. "No, we'll find what we need."

The woman nodded, looked down at Jennifer, who had ignored our nervous scene, and wandered off toward the register again.

"I'm getting out of here," Robyn said.

"Don't huddle over me, all right?" Jennifer said.

"I'm getting out of here," Robyn repeated.

Jennifer stood up. "Just calm down, will you? There's only the lady up there, and she doesn't know what's going on." Her head suddenly swung up to the ceiling. She studied the mirror above us, the entire store was visible in it, but distorted and upended. I wondered if a

2

hidden camera somewhere in the wall panels was monitoring our every movement.
"What about the pharmacist?" Robyn added.
"What about him?"
"Jennifer," I began, "we can't get in trouble. My Mom—"
"You said you would," she interrupted. "Both of you did. You promised. You want your exact words. I thought both of you were more . . . more . . . mature." She emphasized *mature* like she was spitting out nails. Her perfect white teeth made me want to punch her. I couldn't understand why we had agreed to act out this little drama. But Jennifer was an actress, a skillful one who had drawn Robyn and me into thinking we were invisible and could so easily just pick up whatever we wanted and it was ours. Possession was ownership, she had grinned. It was sickening the way her eyes caught both of us, suspended in the twilight blue.
Two little boys came in to poke through the candy. At the rear counter the pharmacist stood up and searched for a prescription on a spindle of papers.
"Besides, you won't get in trouble," Jennifer continued.
"My parents would execute me," Robyn whined.
"Well, only if you got caught."
"That's what I mean." Robyn wheezed slightly, a leftover from years of asthma attacks. I knew when she got excited her breathing became more rapid.
I couldn't understand Jennifer's hypnotic hold over us. I didn't even know why we were standing with her as she debated over the two packages in her hand. Maybe

we were her courage, I thought. Maybe she needed us to prove she would do something that Robyn and I couldn't. She had known all along we wouldn't take anything. Why else would she want to be a normal ninth grader and walk home with *us* when she could have piled into a car full of sophomore boys the way she usually did?

Robyn had decided. She spun abruptly and marched toward the door. Jennifer registered only a brief surprise. "What about you?" Her mouth had become cruel. "Well?"

"We'll wait outside." I didn't bother to see her reaction. Robyn was buying gum when I joined her. As the lady counted out change from a dollar, I tried nonchalantly to pick out Jennifer behind the aisle that obstructed her. But she had ducked down. When we approached the automatic door, I paused as it swung open in front of us. I felt the hair on the back of my neck bristle.

I still couldn't see Jennifer, but I could see the pharmacist. He had a quizzical look on his face. He spun around the counter and strode toward the cosmetic area. Robyn had stopped with me; the warm air from outside swept in the open door against our faces.

And then we saw Jennifer, at least we saw her head. The pharmacist, who looked about eight feet tall, had taken her arm. She shook her head. I wished I could have seen her face. She could make it light up and glow, framed by her blonde hair, curled and feathered, so soft, so perfect. I had seen her switch on often enough for the male teachers when she had failed to produce her homework. She would captivate the sophomore boys when she needed to by smiling, all perfect ivory whites as straight as a row of corn on the cob, and radiating all the warmth she would need for her desired results. Acting came naturally to her.

But she didn't seem to be having much effect on the pharmacist. She was being pulled back reluctantly toward his office.

"Girls, we're not air-conditioning the outside," the cashier said. She watched us, unaware of what was happening at the back of the store.

I pushed Robyn out the door. Stunned, both of us slumped to the curb in front of the drugstore. The late afternoon sun honeyed through the potted trees beside us, and an ocean breeze lifted the call of gulls and the incessant surf from the ocean just two blocks away. A girl clicked past on roller skates.

"Was it your idea or mine?" Robyn finally said.

"I don't know. I should have known when she offered to walk home with us today."

"I sure hope we don't get dragged back in there."

A Porsche convertible idled at the stoplight. The driver, a mid-twentyish businessman, kind of cute, winked at us. I looked down at my sandals until the light changed and he drove away.

"I wonder if he's calling the police?"

"Don't they always for shoplifting?" I asked.

"Weeble, why did we let her talk us into this? She doesn't talk to us at school. She goes by in the hall as if we don't exist. Has she ever sat with us at lunch? Ever?"

"Well, we aren't untouchables."

"I know, but Jennifer the model? Jennifer the actress?

The girl most likely to be Miss America before she graduates?"

"She's not that neat."

"Oh yeah?" she snorted. "Try telling that to any of the male species at school. Ever see Mr. Daniels salivate when she comes into class?"

"He drools over half the girls at school anyway."

We sat silent. The girl on roller skates went by in the other direction clutching a can of pop.

Robyn spotted the police cruiser first. It was coming in the far lane. As it drove past, I expected to see it whirl around and park where we sat, but it nosed on past the beach shops and disappeared.

I was just going to wonder out loud when the drugstore door opened and Jennifer sauntered out. Robyn and I gathered up our books and faced her. Her eyes were smeary—she had been crying—but she smiled at us as if she had just won homecoming queen for the second time that year.

"They're not going to bust you?" Robyn stared, amazed.

"Me?" A coy smile played across her lips. Rehearsed, I realized. "Come on, I'm no criminal."

"And I suppose shoplifting is now a major letter sport." I tried to be sarcastic, but she went right over it.

"Actually . . ." She headed along the sidewalk, us following. "Actually, you would have been pleased with my performance."

I fought down another desire to smack her gorgeous face.

"He was very kind since it was my first offense and everything."

"I bet," Robyn sneered.

"And I, of course, promised to never let such a silly thought like *stealing* happen again."

"Of course," I said.

"Don't tell me." Robyn paraded in front of us. "At first you were shocked and surprised by your unusual behavior. And then tears of embarrassment trickled down your sweet face. Right?" She pranced backward. "Yes, weeping, you triggered feelings of compassion, so he hugged you to his white druggist coat and comforted you. Am I right?"

Jennifer grinned. "Sort of."

I could just imagine the eight-foot pharmacist shrinking in front of Jennifer's wildly blinking eyes until he was a plastic toy man on her palm. There was no need for us to applaud her performance. Not when we had seen it so often.

"Best of all"—she laughed—"he let me keep the makeup."

"You're kidding," I said.

She produced two eye shadows. "I did promise to pay him back when I am able."

"He bought it for you?" I asked. "Unbelievable. You stole the makeup and he lets you keep it? He doesn't even call your parents?"

"He threatened to." She giggled again. "But I can be very persuasive."

We stopped at the intersection for the light to change. The evening traffic had increased. I watched heads swivel toward Jennifer. There was definitely something magical about her, even though I hated it.

"I can't believe you got away with that." Robyn

7

pushed back a stubborn wave of hair. "Geez, that makes me sick."

"Don't be a snit now," Jennifer said. "It was a humiliating experience."

"I'm sure," I said under my breath.

"What's that?"

"Nothing," I muttered and started across the street.

When we reached my street, Robyn turned off with me.

"Aren't you going in my direction?" Jennifer asked.

"Uh, no, I've got to pick up a book from Weeble. An overdue library book she borrowed from me."

Jennifer put her hands on her hips and shrugged. "Okay. Sorry if I spoiled your afternoon."

"Oh no, it was delightful," I lied.

Instead of snapping back, as I would have done, she merely flipped on a couple thousand volts and smiled a dazzling, practiced smile. It disarmed me. I slogged away feeling like warm Jell-O. Robyn caught up.

"Does that make you want to puke, or what?"

Emerald under the western sun, the Pacific shimmered below us as we walked up the ridge of new condos toward my building. Neither of us felt like speaking. The algebra book in my arm was sliding loose. I swung my purse to the other shoulder and adjusted the books.

"Lots of homework?" Robyn asked.

I shook my head. "Nope. I carry them from habit."

She smiled and punched my arm. "Any tests coming up?"

"History."

"Me too." When we reached the steps she stared at me

hard. I had come to recognize that stare as her want-to-talk stare.

As if on cue, she tilted her head back and said, "Want to talk for a while?"

I plopped down onto the steps and gazed out across the rooftops. Two sails bobbed in the distance.

"I wish I had your view," she said.

"Some afternoons," I said dreamily, "the ocean is so blue that the sky blends right in with it; you can't even tell where the horizon is."

"I know." She was breathing heavily from the slight climb up the hill. "Still gonna try out for cheerleading?"

"Probably. If you do."

"I said I would. I haven't been practicing all winter just for my health."

"That's for sure," I chuckled.

"Hey, can I help it if I have allergies. Some people are chubby. Some people have bad skin. Some have icky hair. And I'm lucky to have them all."

"You do not." She was always putting herself down.

"Well, compared to . . ." she stopped. I knew who she was thinking of.

"God I hate girls like that. She doesn't have an honest bone in her body."

"She's popular. She has guys begging to follow her with a ring in their noses. I'd settle for an anonymous phone call once in a while."

"Oh Robyn!"

"Well, I would. You think it was neat last year being voted the eighth-grade girl most likely to be a nun?"

"It was a joke."

9

"For everybody but me. At least you had a boyfriend."

"Me? Who?"

"Scott. And don't deny it, either."

I tried to reassemble Scott's face. He was a blur that mysteriously appeared next to me in English during the middle of eighth grade, all curls and dimples and long, thin hands. I've always liked shy boys, maybe because everybody says I'm kind of shy. But it took three weeks for him to even ask me a question. Still, when he opened up, it had become a comfortable friendship—one of late-night phone conversations about his mother (he didn't have one) and my father (I don't have one) and school and Robyn and his horse, Palomino, who was stabled in the Santa Barbara hills. His dad used to have a ranch, but they moved around quite a bit for some reason he never wanted to talk about. He did promise to take me riding someday, but then he went away over summer vacation and never came back for ninth grade. I sometimes wonder if he really even had a horse.

"Boy, are you getting dreamy." Robyn nudged me. "Thinking about Scott?"

"Yeah. That was my best time."

"It was my loneliest."

"Well, one of these days we'll both have boyfriends and probably be too busy for each other."

I saw my mother's red Mustang swing up the hill. She was early for a change. Maybe the beer company where she was an executive secretary didn't need her as badly as she claimed. I didn't think spending more time with her daughter would cost her job, though to hear her talk, nothing important could happen until she was settled in her sixth-floor office with a chorus of phones ringing like crazy.

"Hi, Kathy!" Robyn was the first to her car. I hung back, trying to decide whether I should tell her about the drugstore incident.

"Hi, Mom," I called. She's told me that I could call her Kathy, too, if I wanted to, because it doesn't make her feel as old as thirty-three—especially with a teenaged daughter—but I prefer Mom.

"Hey kids, what's for dinner? I'm starved."

"Well," I explained, "we just got home and haven't had a chance to—"

"Say no more." She waved off my excuses. "I remember what it's like to be busy with young men pestering you all the way home from school."

I looked at Robyn. She arched her eyebrows and gave me a helpless look. Mom was too preoccupied to notice.

"I gotta get home," Robyn said as I held the door open for her. "Talk to you tomorrow after science."

Mom dug the mail out of our box and hurried up the stairs. Whether it was the bustle of her job or just my mother, she was always in a hurry, impatient to get somewhere. A three-minute egg for her meant two minutes. I've never seen her sit all the way through a movie without jumping up all the time for popcorn or to have a smoke or something. She calls it nervous energy. Well, I've learned to live with her because she's all I've got. And vice versa, at least out here on the West Coast.

"Bills, bills, bills," she groaned and took the steps two at a time. When I reached our open door, she was already scattering her clothes and purse behind her on the floor, searching the cupboards for something that looked appealing and quick for dinner.

I collapsed on the sofa and flung an arm over my eyes.

"What do you want to eat, Weeble dear?"

"Not hungry."

"Now don't start that again. You've got to eat or you'll get sick."

"Spaghetti," I murmured.

"No, the sauce takes too long. I've got to go over some invoices tonight."

"Anything," I said.

She perked up and came into the living room. "I know, let's go out. There's a new Mandarin restaurant just down off of Beach and Laguna. . . ."

I think I agreed as I dropped off to dreams of plastic soldiers marching up my arm to my shoulder and then forcing their way through my ear and into my head, where they warred until Mom shook me awake and told me to go take a nap in my own bed. My snoring was bothering her. So I did.

Two

I was in the laundry room the next day after school, getting a little dizzy from watching my jeans make their three thousandth revolution in the dryer, when a man came in.

He wore a pair of scruffy cutoffs and sandals. He was deeply tanned and kind of cute, except his hair was too short, which made his ears look big.

When Officer Friendly visited my sixth-grade class to tell us about child molesters, he said to remember something prominent about people when you first see them, like a big nose. I guess this guy's ears were pretty prominent, but he didn't look like any kind of molester, maybe just a salesman.

"Got change for a quarter?" he asked me as he dumped a basketful of clothes into a washer.

At first I didn't think he was speaking to me, because he didn't look at me when he spoke, but since I was the only other person in the room, I didn't think he was talking to himself.

"I don't think so," I said as I began to fish around in my purse. "I've got two dimes and five pennies." Actually, I had about a zillion pennies because they seemed to multiply on their own at the bottom of my stuff. But he only needed enough for a quarter, and only the dimes would work in the machines.

"Thanks." He looked at me finally when he gave me the quarter. His eyes were cat green. He knew I was startled by them. "Something wrong?"

I glanced down at my hand and recounted the change. He seemed about my mother's age, maybe a little older. There was a suntan-lotion smell about him, as if he had just come from the beach. He took the change and turned away to set the controls on his machine. There was something attractive about him, in a middle-aged sort of way.

"Hot or warm for cottons," he asked himself. My mother did that sometimes, too. Maybe it was an early stage of being senile.

"Live here?" I ignored his question until he turned and stared at me.

"Yeah, me and my mom."

"Go to school?" I tried to be polite, but I didn't want to encourage him if he was weird or something.

"Uh-huh."

"Married?"

"Me?" It took me a second to realize he was only kidding, but by then he had me, and his smile made me grin too. "Yeah, three kids," I answered.

"Oh?" He was going to play along. "What are their names?"

"Well, there's Flopsy—she's the oldest. And then Mopsy and Cottontail. All girls."

He crossed his arms and leaned against the washing machine. "What about Peter?"

"Peter? Oh, well, he's my husband and father of the girls."

"Thought you lived with your mother?"

He caught me there. "I do—you see, I'm divorced. The girls live with their father."

"Oh . . . uh-huh. I'm divorced too, and I have a boy about your age. Fifteen? He lives with his mother."

Suddenly we weren't talking make-believe anymore, and it wasn't fun. I stared at my jeans, still revolving. He must have sensed I was uncomfortable, because he tried to get me to look at him. "I've seen you walking home from school before. You and another girl, along the Coast Highway, right?"

I nodded.

"And I think you live in the building at the far end of the upper parking lot. Your mother drives a red convertible, and you probably have a messy room."

What he said last worried me. Perhaps he *was* a weirdo who spied on young women and attacked them when they were alone. He must have watched us before to know so much, but how had he known about my room?

I tried not to be obvious about looking at him, but there was a wicked smile on his face, and he knew that I knew he was trying to get a reaction out of me. If that makes any sense.

"Your machine's stopped," he said at last. It had, and I was tempted to grab the jeans and run, but they were too damp. I slid another coin into the slot and clicked the knob. He's only teasing, I thought. Of course he's teasing.

"How do you know all that?" I blurted out.

Before he could answer, though, an old lady came into the room. The man shifted his eyes to her and was silent while she emptied the towels out of her dryer into a plastic clothes basket. Again I thought of leaving, but when my eyes locked with his as the lady muttered something to herself, I realized he wasn't dangerous. It's like how dogs can sense when someone is afraid of them, my intuition. He was harmless after all. I hoped.

"I'm your neighbor—in the building right across," he explained after the woman left. "Name is Tom Pratt."

"Oh." I was a bit more relieved.

"Sometimes I see you coming home and once in a while your mother is on the balcony. And with my telescope . . ."

"What!" Another tease and I had fallen in it like into a bear trap. He grinned again, and for the first time I could see how white his teeth looked against his berry-brown skin.

"Had you going, didn't I?"

"Not really." But it was true, he had. Sometimes it takes me a while to catch on to someone's sense of humor. His was more sly, like this teacher I had once. You could never tell when he was being funny.

He stretched, then flexed his legs like a ballet dancer.

"I did have you going. I bet you thought I was real

strange, a window peeper or something. I live on the first floor, though, and I couldn't see in your apartment if I wanted to."

"But, how did you know about my room?"

"What—being messy? Aren't most teenagers'? My son's is an elephant burial ground, he's got so much junk in it. I just figured you were a normal kid, too."

"It's a little messy," I admitted. I could look directly at him now, like we had broken through a sound barrier. "I don't think I've ever seen your son around here. What's his name?"

"His name is Shawn, and he's never been here. Lives up in San Francisco. With his mother," he added.

"Oh." The conversation hit a dead end again.

"Yeah, he's a good kid. You'd probably like him, too. He has lots of girlfriends but doesn't tie himself down to one. Smarter than his old man. All you kids are, though. Sometimes he amazes me, the things he and his friends come up with. But I don't get to see him as much as I'd like to. He'll be down this summer. If you're around maybe you could . . . No . . ."

"No what?" It drives me crazy when people start a thought and don't finish it. I wasn't going to let him off the hook.

"You've probably got other friends to keep you busy."

"I've got friends, but if you'd like me to show him around or something . . . sure. I'd do it."

"Really?"

He acted surprised, which surprised me. "Is he . . . I mean, what's he look like?"

It was like an inner light went on, the way his eyes

gleamed as he started talking about his kid. He told me all about how he looked—which sounded pretty excellent—and then about the private school he went to and how he had his own sailboat, a Hobi Cat, and he was taking driver education so he could get his license during the summer and maybe a car for his sixteenth birthday, but his mother said that was spoiling him, but his father said so what, if he couldn't spend time with his own son, at least he could spoil him. And on and on. I liked him, and we both sat through the end of our machine cycles until we realized how much time had passed.

I offered him my dryer since I was done with it, and when I left I wanted to say something to him about how I had enjoyed talking but my tongue got all tangled up, so I only said, "See you around."

"Okay—I'll look for you," he said.

Walking back up to our apartment I knew why I felt so happy. For just a little while we each had become what the other needed. It's complicated to explain, but to me it meant that this middle-aged man, who missed his teen-aged son so much it hurt, had been able to imagine I was his kid. And since I didn't have a father, it was easy for me to picture him as my dad. My dad. It didn't hurt me so much, because, as my mom always says, you can't miss what you never had.

But I still had an empty hole inside that just for a little while seemed to have been filled. At least, that's how I tried to explain it to my mom, who was washing her hair in the kitchen sink.

"Can we discuss this later?" she said, her head under the running water of the faucet.

"He was really nice," I repeated for the third time.

"I've warned you about strangers." She was using my shampoo again and had way too much lather in the sink. She always forgot it was a concentrate.

"He seemed so lonely."

"That's worse yet; now don't bother me. I'm late and Roger will be here soon."

"You going out?"

"Just for a while."

"But you said we'd talk later."

"We will."

"When?"

"Tomorrow. He'll be here anytime."

I can't handle it when she's in a hurry—not that she isn't always rushing about anyway—but when she was late it was worse. You just had to get out of her way and let her run whatever was driving her out of her system.

Roger came while she was styling her hair. Still in her bathrobe, she apologized for not being ready, rushed into the bedroom, and left me to pick up the pieces.

"How's school, kid?"

I resented his always calling me a kid. Of all the men my mother dated, Roger seemed like the biggest washout. She had a record for losers—which is maybe why she can talk so knowingly about lonely men—but Roger always made me want to go take a shower and spray the apartment with flea powder after he left.

He had a skinny moustache that never seemed to grow in, wore cowboy boots and some kind of hair grease to slick his sideburns down. On a scale of one to ten, Roger just missed registering on the low end.

"There's tuna salad in the fridge," my mom told me as she flitted out the door. "Get your homework done and don't talk on the phone all night in case I need to call you. Love you, babe." She pecked me on the forehead and was gone.

I went to the window to watch her drive away. The only decent thing about Roger was his car, a silver Camaro. I wished she wouldn't waste time on him or all the Rogers of her life. Why did she have to be a social worker to every lonely man she met? Why couldn't she once bring home someone we could both agree on?

As much as I tried, I couldn't see my mother marrying any of the men she dated. I shuddered just thinking about having to call Roger "Dad."

His car receded into the distance along the Coast Highway. The sun was settling onto the ocean, spinning gold across the surface.

Lights were coming on in apartments across the way. I wondered which one my friend from the laundry room lived in. Funny, I thought to myself, how our apartment complex seemed like a village high on the ocean cliffs. Probably a couple hundred people lived clustered together, but few really knew their neighbors. It was too depressing to dwell on. I went to the refrigerator, more out of duty to my mother than hunger. Later I would call Robyn.

I never got around to Robyn, though. Because I was in one of my occasional mopey moods, I dug out the battered old memory book from the bottom of my sweater drawer. There had been nothing much to record in the past couple months, but something was stirring inside me and I thought putting down some thoughts would help.

As I flipped for an open page, I paused at a photograph of me as a baby. A real chubba-bubba, all fat cheeks and arms with a few wisps of hair curling around my ears. Underneath it was a photo of my mother with her parents and little brother Nicky. They were all squinting into the sun and smiling, so the picture must have been taken a long time ago, before Mom went through her wild stage and had me and was sort of shunned by the family for a while.

On the page next to the photos was a baby tooth under a yellowing piece of tape. I read the child scrawl on the next page, a letter to my father, never sent because no one knew where he was. It was dumb, typical of a five-year-old child, but it made me smile as it brought back long-buried memories.

Someday, I reminded myself, all of this would be important. If I ever met my father, or he found me, I could show him all the memorable events of my life. Most were unimportant and marked only the passing of time, but nevertheless, I recorded them. The days of a life—it sounded like a soap opera.

I rambled on for a couple paragraphs, mainly spacy thoughts about loneliness, a subject I knew pretty well. But some of it was poetic, and it pleased me. "Like the ocean," I wrote, "feelings wash across the sand dunes in my memory. Under the endless surge of foam are shells and driftwood and dead sea creatures. They roll in with the tide and soon disappear. But they are not forgotten."

I really liked the part where I said, "And inside of me

nothing is forgotten. Stored among the shells and drift pieces of my life are treasures, worn smooth by the sea. Someday . . ." and I trailed off because my brain had stalled in mid-thought.

The phone rang. I hoped it might be my film agent to tell me he wanted me in his next movie, but it was only my mom's friend Bob. He was a mortician who wore glasses that turned a weird tint like sunglasses, so you could never see his eyes. Even my mom thought he was too creepy to go out with, but he sometimes got us concert tickets for free. I don't know how he got them; he never explained and we never asked.

When he hung up I thought of calling Robyn but it was too late. I wandered back into my room but couldn't think of anything else to say in my memory book.

I flipped through last year's school yearbook, searching out all the cute guys I'd never go out with because I was just a blur in the halls to most of them. There were a couple I had a chance with, but I couldn't just barge up and say I'm available. When I was younger I would kiss a favorite picture I had of Donny Osmond, and I was tempted to kiss a couple pictures in my yearbook, but that seemed a little hard-up and retarded, even though I was alone.

Being alone didn't bother me, but being alone and bored was a pain. I turned off the lights in my room and sat at the window watching cars weave a necklace of taillights past the beach shops. Lots of people had somewhere to go, or maybe, like me, they were just trying to find a way to pass the boredom.

Three

Cheerleading tryouts were going to be tough this year. Robyn and I vowed to make it or we would jump off the end of the Newport pier together. We both knew I had the best chance since I had made the eighth-grade squad last year and knew the cheers and all. She knew them too, but when people see you in your uniform all year, they kind of take it for granted that you'll make cheerleading again.

But I didn't want to discourage Robyn. She had practiced all winter until her parents had to set aside certain times for her to cartwheel and shout and be interruptive.

As we stood outside the gym waiting for the boys' basketball team to finish their spring drills, I surveyed the group of anxious candidates. I knew most of the girls. Some had older sisters who were now tenth and eleventh graders, and were cheerleaders. That was an advantage. Since a group of teachers made the final decision on the tryouts, it helped to have your name confused with your older sister who had been cheerleading captain or most valuable cheerleader. I wasn't so lucky.

"My legs are turning to sponge, Weeble," Robyn moaned.

"Not for the preliminaries. All you have to do is go out and do the cheers with the whole group. You don't even need to show walkovers or handsprings."

"But what if I get next to Shelly or one of the Anderson twins or somebody who moves like a Dallas Cowgirl?"

"Robyn!" It was easy to get exasperated with her. "There are fifty people trying out. You've got to be pretty bad not to make the first cut."

There was a commotion over near the gym doors. The basketball team had been dismissed, and they began to trickle through the sprawl of girls. I recognized most of the players, but in such a crush of bodies, no one stopped to talk. I saw Jennifer hugging one of the cute starters. She could be like Old Faithful the way she gushed forth her affection.

I had successfully avoided her the past two days after her shoplifting spree. The way she was going on over the guy whose neck she had her arms wrapped around, I could tell she had recovered from the incident, too. Boy had she. She even kissed him on the cheek—more to get a reaction from him and his friends who kept jostling him to move on than for any other reason. Robyn's theory was that we were jealous of all the male attention she got, which, deep down, I didn't want to admit might be true.

I grabbed up the old pom-poms and elbowed my way into the gym. The smell of sweat still hung in the air. The basketball coach conferred with two of his players in the middle of the floor, but when they saw the girls filing in, they drifted off to a far corner.

I was stiff at first. My back felt like a hunk of gum when you first pop it into your mouth. The more I worked it, the more supple it became. I measured my hips and thighs against the girls nearest to me. I was in pretty good shape. Not that I try to be athletic, but keeping up with my mom would make anyone skinny.

Robyn slapped her buns. "Pretty firm, huh?"

"I guess. What's your secret, aerobic exercises?"

"Negative thinking."

I couldn't help but laugh. "No, I'm not making fun of you, it's just that . . . well . . . negative thinking makes sense."

"With me you mean," she said, frowning. "The secret is to hate and despise fat, you know, send negative thought impulses to the parts of your body where fat grows, and then the fat will feel unwanted and melt away. It's my new system."

"It must work." I grinned.

"I think I'll patent it." She was serious, I think.

I watched her warm up. After about a minute of bending and rolling her shoulders and straining her legs out to the side, her face turned red. She really looked as if she was struggling, but I knew she wouldn't admit it. That's another thing I liked about her. She might put herself down all the time, but she was so stubborn, she never gave up at anything.

I closed my eyes and listened to her huff. A wheeze like a faraway train whistle rattled out of her chest. Someone tittered behind me. I heard snatches of one girl giving advice to another about trying out braless with a tight leotard. She guaranteed that it had worked for her last spring.

"Can we have some music, Carl?" Mrs. Williams called up to the pressbox. Carl the Cruel—that's what everybody called him, although I'm not sure why—waved and switched on the PA speakers. An upbeat tune blared and echoed in the cavernous gym. Carl seemed to enjoy supervising the warm-ups. Other than a janitor who mopped the floor, he was the only male present.

I think maybe he used to shock the white mice in the biology lab when he was in seventh grade. I recalled rumors of him splicing a twelve-volt battery to the mice and then watching them hop convulsively until they burnt out. Anyway, it was Carl the Cruel, as if no one remembered he had a last name.

"God, I hope I don't have cramps." Robyn interrupted my daydreams. "My body is so unpredictable lately."

I stood up and exhaled. "You don't feel well?"

"My head says one thing and my body another."

I was a little fluttery myself. And I didn't want to nursemaid Robyn now. "Ignore the pain."

"That's what my mom always says. You know, I can't figure out this conspiracy: every time something important comes up, my body goes all out of whack."

"Just nerves."

"My dad says that. But take the Christmas concert for instance. Remember? I'm supposed to do a duet with

Missy and that morning I break out with hives all over my neck and face. My dad says it's nerves. My doctor says it's an allergic reaction. My body turns against me, just when I really need it."

"You sound paranoid."

"What's that mean?"

"I don't know, but when I start complaining, my mom says I'm paranoid, and it shuts me right up."

"Really? Maybe I'll try that when my mom starts yakking at me to clean up my room."

"All right girls, attention please." Mrs. Williams waved her clipboard in the air. As girls' gym instructor, it was her responsibility to organize the tryouts every year. She knows all the cheers and tries to demonstrate them herself, but it always reminds me a little of a giraffe trying to tap-dance. She's too gangly to be graceful. Besides, in a group of teenage girls, she looks out of place doing splits.

One time I was following the sidewalk along the beach and this really sexy lady in a bikini whizzed by on skates. Then she looped and skated back by me. When she was right alongside I could see she was tan and in really super condition, but her face belonged to a fifty-year-old. She was that old but trying to be an adolescent. Mrs. Williams is a little like that. My mom too, now that I think about it.

After everyone had signed in on the clipboard, we had to limber up in formation and go through a little dance routine while Carl kept pushing his glasses back onto his nose and replaying the same record.

"Everybody loose?" Mrs. Williams signaled two girls

to step forward and demonstrate the first cheers we would all do. The first was a basic *Go team*, the second a simple rhythm of *We've got the power, we've got the steam*, except the trick is to shuffle faster and faster to imitate a locomotive.

I liked the third cheer because I could leap up and splay my head and arms back. I always felt a little like an eagle taking off, except I came back down too soon.

Robyn was keeping up well. I watched her from the corner of my eye. As the movements became more difficult she gritted her jaws together and tried to maintain perfect execution.

Some of the experienced girls up front were goofing off: this was no challenge for them. They didn't feel the same pressures that the girls trying out for the first time did.

Even though I had made the squad last year, I could remember the fear, the tightness across my chest. I knew most of the group would be rejected. I had cried myself last year, even though I had been selected. But those that hadn't were devastated. If Robyn failed to last the cuts, I would feel responsible for goading her all winter to practice, practice, telling her it would be a cinch to make it.

Jennifer's group had wandered over to the drinking fountain. Her three friends were as lithe and confident as she. I expected Mrs. Williams to order them back into the herd, but she just glanced their way and continued making checks on her clipboard.

After about twenty minutes we broke to rest. A few of the basketball players had returned after their showers and were now loitering around the door. I slipped past them and ran down toward the bathrooms.

The face in the mirror was flushed. My hair always frizzed when I was hot. The National Science Foundation comes around every year to show off their energy inventions, and some kid always volunteers to put his hand on a generator so a million volts can pulse through his body. His hair always stands up from the electricity. That's how mine looked. My stomach looked lumpy. I usually skip lunch, but I go berserk for pizza burgers. I regretted my addiction as I bent over the sink and slapped cold water on my cheeks.

Robyn was waiting for me in the hall. Actually, she was gaping at a couple who had chosen the stairs to make out on. I'm not against public displays of affection, but I had to avert my eyes as his hand snuck under her T-shirt. Robyn wasn't quite as polite.

"Let's go sit down," I suggested.

"Gosh, next they'll be shooting skin flicks in the halls."

I tweaked her arm. "You're just jealous."

"Maybe I am."

"Robyn!" I pretended to scold her, but she nudged me and pointed down the hall. Mr. Blair, our history teacher, had been cornered by a group of girls. Way back in seventh grade Robyn and I had voted Mr. Blair as the teacher we would most like to be marooned with. Our feelings hadn't changed.

"Let's go talk to him," she said.

"Not like this. We look like cheerleaders from the black hole. Besides, he's busy."

"What? He's just talking."

"He's a flirt."

"So what? He's a judge too. It won't hurt to remind him that his top history students are slaving for the good of Oceanside High. You know, appeal to his school spirit." She grabbed my arm and dragged me forward.

"Don't prejudice my voting now." He winked at us as we came up. "My judgments can't be swayed."

"No amount of money?" Robyn joked.

He crossed his arms and squinted at us. "I'm impartial. Unless of course you both ace the next history test."

"Is that a gray hair?" I teased him whenever I could.

He removed a long blonde hair from his shirt. "Obviously not mine."

"Uh-huh." I wagged my finger at him. "Looks like one of Miss Fritz's." Miss Fritz was one of the art teachers.

"Well, we had a faculty meeting after school," he said. I studied his face for the grin that was imminent. He was easy to talk to. I used to have a real crush on him, as I'm sure every girl who was in his classes did, but now I just like him as a friend. And a teacher.

"When are you going to ask my mom out?"

He stared at me puzzled. "Was I going to?"

"That's right, I'm a witness," Robyn broke in. "You met her at the homecoming dance—you were chaperones together, remember?"

He stroked his cheek. "A little short lady, very attractive, talks fast?"

"Uh-huh," I said. "You danced with her all night. Don't try to be innocent with us."

"I confess." He threw up his hands. "How is your mother?"

"She's fine." I tried to be solemn. "Actually, she's very lonely and wakes up at night calling out your name. I keep telling her that you've promised to ask her out, but you know how scorned women are."

He stared at me wide-eyed, then his face relaxed. He knew us too well not to recognize our teasing. "Soon, very soon. I've written a note somewhere"—he began searching through his pockets—"about calling your mother for dinner."

Robyn shook my arm, alarmed. "They've started again."

We waved over our shoulders as we dashed back into the gym. Mrs. Williams was calling out the final eliminations. Each person had to do a required cheer and jump, although I didn't know the sense of having everyone do the routines all at once. I suppose so no one would be too nervous.

Mr. Blair was peeking in the door, curious. He would be just right for my mother, I reflected. Not too tall, almost the same age—no, I think he was just thirty-two, which would have made him a year younger. But what's a year? Yes, I could picture them together.

My concentration wasn't on the last set. Everyone milled around afterward and discussed who the obvious standouts were. Robyn dangled her arms forlornly, as if she was certain her name wouldn't appear on the bulletin board in the morning along with the chosen ones.

"Everybody makes the preliminary cut," I tried to assure her.

"I blew it Weeble, I know I blew it."

"You didn't! Come on, I'll walk you home." We didn't

like to shower at school. The shower room was too much like a meat market, with everyone comparing and sizing you up to make sure you didn't think you were neater than you really were. I never could understand why girls have to search out each other's flaws with such determination.

"Why did I let you talk me into trying out?" She was still dejected. I loped along next to her, my damp T-shirt sticking against me.

"It's your negative thinking again. You've got to believe you'll make it. You were as good as anybody I saw."

"Really? You noticed me then?"

"Of course. I watched you the whole time, and your jumps were strong, you had fluid movements. Don't worry, okay?"

"You really think so?" She brightened up. I could usually snap her out of moodiness. I was almost impossible to boost once I got depressed, but she had more swings of mood than I could imagine. "You know," I continued, "I can tell you've been working hard the last couple of months. You've slimmed down."

"You can tell? I did lose eight pounds since the first of the year. I bet we even weigh about the same now, huh?"

We turned off busy Tropic Boulevard and cut across a field under construction. A small shopping center was about ready to open, once the parking lot was poured. To the west, the ocean shattered against the sea rocks. On impulse, I headed toward the beach road.

"How come you're going that way?" Robyn asked.

"I need to cool off."

"Fine with me." Even though it was approaching dinnertime, neither of us had to be home promptly. Robyn huffed as she tried to keep up.

With the exception of a jogger running his collie, the beach was deserted. A scraggly gull pecked away on a dead fish. Driftwood piled against the lifeguard stand. The water froze our legs in no time: the temperature was still only about sixty degrees. In another month, by mid-June at the latest, it would be tolerable for swimming.

A sloop rocked just beyond the jetty.

"Wish that was my boat," Robyn said wistfully.

"But your parents already have a gigantic sailboat."

"*They* do, *I* don't. They never let me use it."

"Could you if you wanted to?"

"Oh, I don't know." She stooped and gathered a handful of the gritty sand. "Probably not. David could, but he's in college so I guess they trust him. Tell you the truth"—she paused and flung the sand toward the surf—"Weeble, things aren't so good at home. Lots of fights lately and Mom gets drunk every night. Well, not drunk really, but she's always carrying around a drink. She can hold her alcohol pretty good. But some nights my father doesn't even come home."

"Really?"

"Yeah, convenient business trips, you know. Parents can be so dumb sometimes, just like little kids."

I was too thoughtful to reply. More and more, there were times when I felt as if I was the mother and my mom was the daughter. If that makes any sense. Sometimes she acted like fifteen and I felt like I was in my thirties.

But Robyn had the ideal family. Two children, a successful father who spoiled her, a mother who could model for *Vogue*. Maybe her negative thinking was taking over again. I splashed back out into the water. Far out I could see an ocean liner steaming north for San Pedro Harbor. Where was it from? The Orient? Australia? Maybe Europe? All that free, open ocean in front of me and I couldn't go anywhere. When I turned back to shore, I could tell Robyn had been crying. She sniffled and wiped her eyes.

"This sea air always affects my allergies," she mumbled.

"At least you have a mother and a *father*," I said at last. "Even though he's not perfect, he's better than none at all."

"Sometimes I wonder," she said. A handful of sand trickled through her fingers.

I put my arm around her shoulder as we started up the hill that led to the shops. "Robyn," I said. "If I had a sister, I'd want her to be just like you."

She blinked shyly. "Really?"

"Yep. And if I had a father, I'd want him to be just like Robert Redford." And then I tripped her into the sand.

"Oh you!" She struggled to her feet and chased after me.

But I knew, and she knew, there was something serious in what I had said. She was special, even with her wacky weight-reduction theories of negative thinking.

Four

My mother detached my headphone plug. Instead of hearing Michael Jackson, there was only a faint hum, as I lay sprawled on my furry rug.

"Right in the middle. What'd you do that for?" I growled.

"I need your help for a minute." She yawned. "I've got to move the sofa and chairs before I go to bed. We're getting new carpet in the morning, and I have to finish cleaning."

I sat up to my knees. "If we're getting new carpet, why are you cleaning now? That doesn't make sense."

She looked tired. "Don't argue," she said. "Just come."

I followed her into the living room. Two end tables and the lamps and plants were piled in one corner of the room. The vacuum cord snaked across the floor. The sundeck window was open, and sounds from a small party drifted up from below.

"Is that those guys in two-oh-two again?"

She looked at me with a weary So what?

"Why don't they party on weekends like everyone else? They always have to pick an off night to keep me awake."

"Close your window and you won't hear them," she said.

"Sure, and then I suffocate."

"Just grab that end," she said as she bent over to grasp the bottom of the sofa. I slid my hand under the other end and promptly pinched my fingers.

"Ow! Wait 'til I get a good hold."

She sighed, exasperated. "I've never seen such a ninety-eight-pound weakling."

"Ninety-four," I corrected her.

We tried again. This time she lugged and I grunted until we had slid the cumbersome sofa where she wanted it. I stood at the window and stared out. "Keep it down!" I called.

"Weeble, don't be inconsiderate."

"Me? They're the ones that are disturbing us. Tell *them* not to be inconsiderate."

"It's early yet."

"Almost eleven!" I collapsed on the sofa. I knew my mom agreed with me about the noise, but she would go out of her way not to let anybody know. Especially since they were young singles. As if the singles in our building should live by different rules, I thought.

"Now the chairs," she said.

"Can't you move them yourself?"

She looked down at me, a dull expression in her droopy eyes. She was in an I-don't-want-to-fight mood.

Instead of admitting she was tired and going to bed, she pretended to be peppy. But weariness poked through all over her.

"Fine, I'll do it myself," she finally said.

Her martyr complex, I realized. "All right, all right. I just can't figure out why we have to move everything when the carpet men could easily move it all in the morning. Plus they'll probably leave a mess." She ignored what I had said. "And if you won't go down and knock on two-oh-two's door and tell them that people are trying to sleep, I will."

She rubbed her eyes. Here comes the I-am-your-mother bit, I thought. "Weeble, I *am* your mother, and I would like you to respect that fact. It doesn't make it any easier to go around alienating the neighbors, especially since we have to live here, too."

I struggled to my feet and in wild-eyed frenzy shoved both chairs and the ottoman next to the sofa. Then I strode back into my room and slammed the door. My mom always has a way of making play seem like work and work like sheer drudgery. I plugged back into Barry Manilow. A full orchestration swept around me. I closed my eyes and tried to replay the hectic day. Cheerleading tryouts. Robyn's parents. Mr. Blair promising for the umpteenth time to take Mom out. Another month of school. The swirl of music seemed to come from all about me, a whirlpool of violins, and Barry's voice gentling me.

I reached under my dresser and pulled out a crumpled sheet of note paper that I noticed there. My uneven scrawl in bold print read **Get Your Head On Straight**. I didn't remember when I had written that.

I also retrieved the silver post to an earring that

had fallen into the rug. I could see a whole flock of teen magazines under my bed. I dug out my scrapbook. *"To Elizabeth, on her seventh birthday. Love, Grandma and Grandpa,"* it said in Grandma's squiggly handwriting. The binding was torn. I carefully folded over the first page.

There I was, a plump partridge on Grandpa's lap. The picture next to it was of my mother in her swimming suit, but when we still lived in Indiana. A lake in the background I didn't recognize. I wondered why I wasn't in that picture. Another snapshot of me, and one where I was eating sand. Yuk. My mouth looked like a garbage disposal.

A picture of me in a party dress in front of a cake. Underneath Mother had written, *"Elizabeth, fourth birthday."* I studied my glazed expression. What was I thinking then? It was a year before we moved to California. It might have been the summer Grandma's black cat jumped on my head and clawed my neck. It was when I was still Elizabeth.

Elizabeth. It struck me as funny. Nobody at school would know who Elizabeth Miller was. But Weeble? Sure, Weeble—even the teachers knew that. One of my mom's first toys to me was a little roly-poly Weeble doll that rolled over and sprang back up—just like me when I started to walk. Topsy-turvy Weeble.

A snapshot of me being hugged by Minnie Mouse at Disneyland. How old? Nine?

Every day Mom drove by the spires of the Matterhorn at Disneyland on her way to work in Anaheim—every day—and she rarely glanced over to see Disneyland, the magic kingdom, the place where all weeble children are children forever.

I resented Mom's passing by so close and seeing only the bumper of the car in front, the freeway snarled with motorists ornery to get where they were going. Oh well, I rationalized, it was her job. Maybe I wouldn't appreciate the beauty either if I had to choke in exhaust.

I didn't hear Mom knock at the door. It must have been slight, because the song on the stereo was a mellow one. She tapped me on the shoulder. I lifted the headphones.

"It's getting late." A sincere smile. She recognized the photo album on the floor. "Poring over your childhood?"

"Yeah. Trying to remember what Grandma and Grandpa look like. It's been three years since they came out to visit."

"I know." My mom missed them, too, but if she kept busy enough she wouldn't have to think sad thoughts. Not me. I think best when I can work myself into a sad mood. "Better get to bed." She kissed me on the forehead and went out in a ruffle of blue terrycloth. "Oh, I forgot to tell you." She stuck her head back in and withdrew a postcard from her robe. "A card was mixed in with the bills." She handed it to me.

A glossy picture of a giant ear of corn was on one side. I looked at the signature on the other. It was from Nicky, Mom's twenty-five-year-old brother.

"He's coming out for a visit," she said and smiled.

"Really!" I read the note with excitement. He had split with his rock group and he wanted to try the West Coast. He thought he could find a lead or rhythm-guitarist job with a recording studio, and he would be flying in on Saturday. I had only Thursday and Friday to get ready! Two days to remember his laughing face peering at mine. He had taught me to ride a bike. He had teased me silly. My only uncle, and he was coming. I felt like whooping.

"Now calm down and get to sleep," Mom said. And then she was gone.

I held the card and reread it. Nicky! His face was a mixed-up jumble of colors. He always smelled clean, like soap. And his hair, when I remembered it, had a sweet scent to it, like pinecones.

I never failed to get a Christmas card from him and a crisp two-dollar bill each birthday. But it had been so long, over seven years since his high school graduation when Mom surprised me and we flew back to Indiana. And before then? My memory seemed all out of focus. We visited once when I was in first or second grade. That's when Nicky taught me to ride a bike, but since then Mom was always too busy to get time off, and no one back there ever seemed to want to come all the way to California to see us. Nicky got busy with his music and my grandparents just got old, I guess.

I slipped into my nightgown and climbed between the cool floral sheets. There was so much to show him, so much to talk about. Next to Mom, he was my only other link to a fuzzy and faraway childhood in Fort Wayne. I'd spent the first five years of my life there, and Mom had grown up there. And yet I knew so little about it.

Some nights I tossed sleepless in bed and tried to imagine Grandma's enormous old house. There had been a porch swing. A dusty attic. An ancient root cellar with jars of pickles and beets and tomatoes. I couldn't remember much. But it was enough to hold on to.

I rolled over, my head burning with thoughts. There was Mom standing in the moist cut grass. And I tagged after her. And a man? I tried to bring him into focus. I wanted to so much. But I couldn't. The image faded out, and finally, I slept.

Five

The cheerleading results were posted the next morning. Thirty-eight girls still remained in the contention for six cheerleading spots. My name was the fourth from the top. I scanned the list quickly as a girl behind me pushed forward to see the names. I elbowed her back. "Wait a second, okay?"

I read through the list again. Robyn's name was second from the bottom. Relieved, I went to find her. She was too knotted up to check for herself.

She was sitting on the front lawn under the flagpole, her head down as I came up. "Some bad news, Robyn." It was the wrong thing to say. She looked up at me like she was going to cry. "No, really, I was just kidding."

"You mean . . ."

"You made it," I announced.

"Oh my God." She collapsed back on the grass. "I do believe in miracles."

I plunked down beside her. "I told you all along that you'd make the first cut. You *were* good. Now we have to work twice as hard for the finals."

She grimaced. "Maybe I should just quit now and be satisfied with getting this far. You know, save myself the humiliation of getting axed."

"No way!" A bus began unloading in the circle drive. "No, we're in this together. All the way, remember!"

"That's what Bonnie said to Clyde right before they bit the bullet," she groaned.

I dragged her to her feet. Algebra was about to begin, and I wanted to compare homework with her before everyone arrived. "Come on. I've got some tremendous news to tell you on the way to class."

"Mrs. Armentrout died?" A wicked smile pulled at the corners of her mouth. People who didn't know Robyn better might think she was cruel. But we were about the only two people in the whole school who tolerated the daffy old librarian, Mrs. Armentrout. I had even heard other teachers make fun of her eccentricities.

"No, better than that." I tried to keep one eye on who was walking with who as we moseyed toward the math building. New romances sprung up and died out so quickly that a Las Vegas bookie could make a fortune betting on the brief unions.

"Nicky? Did you ever show me a picture of him?" she asked after I had explained about the postcard.

"I think so, but the most recent picture was his high school graduation seven years ago. He's either twenty-five or twenty-six now."

"Really? Is he cute?"

"He's a Miller, isn't he? Anyway, he's my uncle, so be realistic."

"Well . . ." The wicked grin again. "You're a Miller and look at you! And he may be your uncle, but he's fair game for me."

We picked out desks near the front of the room. It was a muggy morning, and there was very little breeze. The wooden seats were already sticky. I dug out my assignment on integers and began rechecking it.

"How long is he going to stay?" Robyn was fidgeting with a small mirror and comb.

"I don't know. Depends on if he finds a job or not, I guess."

She tried to smooth down an unruly curl that flipped back. "What kind?"

"Huh?" I went over the same problem for the third time.

"What kind of job?"

"Oh." I glanced up as two boys strolled by my desk. One of them craned his neck to see what I was working on. He carried no books or folders, so I assumed he had no homework either. Robyn was looking at me goggle eyed.

"Am I distracting you?"

"What did you say?" I asked her.

"Just let me see your homework," she growled and snatched my paper. Her paper was smudged with erasures.

"Nicky"—I picked up my thread of thought again—"is a rock guitarist. Pretty good too. He sent us a cassette tape of himself last Christmas. He wants to hook up with a group or a recording studio, if he can."

"Really?" She stopped and appraised me, obviously impressed. "A rock musician."

"For sure," I said. "All us Millers have talent."

She didn't reply. The second bell rang and then class began. My mind wasn't going to be on school that day. All I could think about was Nicky coming. Would he have changed? I knew that I had, but my mom didn't like to admit it. But how would it be having a man in the house, even if he was only my uncle? It was always just me and my mom, just the two of us.

A whole squadron of butterflies rose in my stomach. Two days, I told myself, was forty-eight hours, was 2,880 minutes, was . . .

I was home that evening flipping television channels when Robyn called.

"Can I come over?" A tiny voice, distant. "Something happened. Is it okay?"

"Sure, I'm not doing anything." Alarm crept over me. I can usually sense when something is wrong, and after Robyn hung up my hands started shaking. Everyone says I'm real tuned into feelings. I'd make a good gypsy fortune-teller if I ever saw a job advertised in the classifieds.

Mom was in her bedroom sorting through papers when Robyn arrived. Robyn led me into my bedroom, and after I had closed the door, she burst into tears. I tried to comfort her, but sometimes it's best to let a person get everything out of her system. This was one of those times.

She finally calmed down a bit and blubbered, "They had a big fight."

"Your parents?" She nodded. "About what?"

"Same old stuff," she sniffled. "You know, he's never home, and then he calls her a pig with her snout always in a bottle of gin, and she swears at him. You know." Her shoulders shook as she tried to take a breath. I stroked her hair.

"That happens between people sometimes."

She broke into sobs again. "It's all the time with my parents. And they won't even listen to me."

"You tried to talk to them?" She nodded again. "What'd they say?"

"Butt out. Go to your room. Like that."

I sat down next to her on the bed and helped her stare at the floor. I wanted to be wise and comforting, but parents baffled me. Especially since I'd only had experience in mothers. "Did they get physical?"

"A little," she shrugged. "My mom sees how far she can push before he storms out of the house. Then she usually throws a few ashtrays against the wall. I can't stand listening to them."

"No," I said softly. "I imagine you wouldn't."

"But, I can't ignore it. God, they're my parents after all."

"Did you think about calling David?"

She wiped her nose with the back of her hand. The more we talked, the more she began to relax. "Naw. He's up in Santa Barbara. Why would he care? I tried to tell him once when he was home that Mom and Dad fought all the time, but he said that's just normal. But I don't think it is," she said emphatically.

"I don't either." I listened to her breathing slow. In another minute she exhaled and shook back her hair.

"Oh, I don't know, Weeble. I shouldn't dump all my problems on you."

"I don't mind," I protested. "It's good training for when I grow up and become a psychiatrist."

She looked at me and forced a smile. I wanted to have her talk everything out, but I didn't want to pry into uncomfortable areas. There was a rap on the door. Mom peeked in, surprised to see Robyn.

"I didn't hear you sneak in. What are you two plotting?"

"Nothing. Robyn's parents just had a fight tonight, and I'm helping her get straight," I blurted out.

Robyn glanced sheepishly at my mother. "It's not unusual," she said.

"I'm sorry to hear that. Can I do anything?" My mother would make a great social worker if she ever decided to give up her big salary and penthouse office. She really does care about helping people. One time she brought home a little Mexican woman to stay with us for two weeks. I think the woman got deported for not having her immigration papers, though.

"I should probably get back home." Robyn started to get up.

"You can stay with us tonight if you want," Mom offered. "I'll be happy to call your mother and check with her."

"You're sure it's all right?" She looked at my Mom hopefully.

"It's all settled, then," I agreed. I searched through my closet for a sleeping bag. After I had unrolled it next to my bed and Robyn had kicked off her jeans, Mom returned to say that it was OK. She thought she had awakened Mrs. Johnson, but Robyn said she gets that way when she's drinking.

I went to get a couple of Cokes for us out of the refrigerator. Robyn was doodling with my sketch pad when I came back. I wondered if she still wanted to talk about her parents.

"I think they're going to get a divorce," she said offhandedly.

That startled me. I put her bottle down on the floor. I wanted to smooth away the pain I saw in her face. She squinted at the outline of a tree and then scribbled over it, dissatisfied.

"Maybe they'll work it out," I suggested.

"I doubt it." She began a house. She put squiggles coming out of the chimney and then a smiling face in one of the upstairs windows. The face had two pigtails that hung down on each side. She scratched it out.

"Have they gotten help from anyone?"

"My parents?" she snorted. "I told them they should just *call* a marriage counselor, but they both looked at me like I was an alien-speaking Martian or something. I think they'd rather pretend there's no problem."

"Doesn't anybody else know?" I sipped my pop and watched her start a horse with a dog face. Its tail looked like a fifth leg. Art has never been one of her top subjects.

"I don't see how our neighbors can help but know. They just talk and wave and go on like everything is normal, though. What really makes me mad is a couple of weeks ago my father brought home a business associate, you know, someone to impress. And everybody just acted so friendly. My dad pecks my mom on the cheek and she smiles and they chat with after-dinner drinks. And this guy is no sooner backing out the drive than Dad is snapping at Mom and she runs into their bedroom and locks the door. Can you believe it? And I have to live in the middle of this."

I searched hard for a solution. She hadn't touched her Coke yet.

"You want to hear my new Billy Joel record?" I asked.

She didn't respond. I thought back to the most recent fight I had with my mother. Usually we skipped over our disagreements soon after they occurred. But not too long ago I knew Mom was wrong about partying out late with a couple of friends without calling me. When she says what time she'll be home and then doesn't show, I get worried. Especially when she doesn't call. I can't sleep very well when I'm all alone. And I haven't had a babysitter in two or three years. When I nagged her about it she exploded and called me some nasty names about being a baby and like that. Well, I didn't mean to, but I tipped over a bowl of cereal, and she thought I did it on purpose. I stormed off to school barefoot. When I got home, there was a bouquet of flowers and an apology note. I put the flowers in my room and never said anything about them when she came home. She never said anything about the fight or staying out late. That was that.

I clicked on the turntable and adjusted the volume on the record. It occurred to me as I sat back on the bed that maybe upbeat music would have been better for Robyn.

She rolled over to her back and shielded her eyes from the light. I felt like I was at the Humane Society watching abandoned puppies through wire bars. I hate helpless feelings.

"Do you ever think about having a father?" she asked.

"All the time," I replied. "I love my mom, but she's busy and . . . you know . . . only one person."

"Do you remember much about him?" She kept her eyes closed and waited for me to continue. We'd never really talked about it before. She, like everyone else, just assumed that my parents had gotten divorced when I was little and that I didn't like to discuss it. I tried to find the right words. Why are the right words always so elusive?

"I don't remember." I paused.

She looked up at me. "Nothing?"

"The truth is Robyn, my mom never was married." A hollowness stirred deep inside me. The essential puzzle piece to complete the picture was lost, undeniably gone. I fought down a vague longing.

"Does it bother you?"

"No—well, just a little. Like a vaccination in the arm, you know. It hurts a little, but it fades away. *I* can't do anything about it." I watched her eyes. They were curious with their cocker-spaniel sadness about them.

"How come they didn't get married?"

"My mom says that both of them agreed it would have been a mistake. They weren't compatible. No one consulted me."

"So you never knew him?"

"Nope. He moved to Texas right before I was born.

I've thought about writing him or trying to find his telephone number, but Mom says he had a habit of moving around quite a bit. It's funny though, once when I was about seven and real interested in knowing about him, she got kind of misty, choked up. I think she was imagining what it would have been like if they had married."

"Geez, it must be hard knowing he's still alive somewhere and you can't even see him. Your own father." She wrinkled up her face, concerned. "At least I've got both my parents, even though they'd like to kill each other most of the time."

I suddenly realized how futile it was to try to solve Robyn's problem. Because of the way I was raised, I certainly didn't know what a normal marriage was. I listened to Billy Joel sing about emptiness; he should have consulted me.

"I'm sure they both love you, Robyn," I said out of the blue. I didn't know what prompted the thought. She gazed at me. After an awkward silence she rolled over and asked me to switch off the light.

Shadows patterned the wall from the streetlamp. The neighborhood was quiet; only an occasional car revved up on the Coast Highway blocks away. I wanted to say more to Robyn, but I couldn't think of anything appropriate.

After a bit I whispered, "Just wait. You'll like Nicky." I glanced over at her, but she was sleeping peacefully.

Six

When I arrived home after school the next day, a guy in his early twenties was sitting on the steps of our building. I started to step over his suitcase and guitar case when I realized it was Nicky.

"Nicky?"

"Little Elizabeth?" He stood up. He was gorgeous. Tall and thin, toffee brown hair, and eyes so blue they looked bottomless. He gave me a hug that lifted me two feet off the ground. His cheek smelled like licorice.

"We didn't expect you until tomorrow. Does Mom know you're here?"

"No." A penetrating smile. "I got an early flight out, and rather than wait around the airport, I caught a taxi over. I thought I'd surprise you. My God, are you growing up!" He stepped back and examined me. I blushed.

I led him into our building and then lugged his guitar case up three flights of stairs. When I pushed open our apartment door, a majestic view of the ocean was the

52

first thing he saw. He whistled low. "Wow. We sure don't have any vistas like that in Fort Wayne."

"I bet. You hungry? Want anything to drink?"

He shook his head, then took my hand and pulled me over to the sofa. "I can't believe I'm really here."

"Me neither." I had so much to say that the words just jammed up in my throat. I stared at him with a gawky expression and hoped he would talk first. The change in him since the last time I'd seen him was dramatic. Not only had he let his hair grow, but his face was fuller, his eyes sparkly. And when he laughed again, I felt the astonishment and warmth he had brought into the room.

"I am just knocked over by you, Elizabeth."

I crinkled up my nose. "Weeble. Everybody calls me Weeble."

"Still?" He hugged me to him. I wasn't sure how to react. I think I was a little stiff. He leaned back and asked me to tell all about what was happening in my life.

I began hesitantly, but within a few minutes I was rattling on in a nonstop avalanche of words, retelling about school and Mom's job and my friends and things I was sure I had mentioned a hundred times in letters, but he nodded and encouraged me to continue. I was midpoint in a long story about our weird neighbors that we suspected of having connections to organized crime, when the front door opened. Mom dropped her purse when she saw Nicky, and then he was lifting her into the air and twirling her around the room. When she finally got free and stopped laughing, she slumped onto the sofa next to me and watched Nicky pace about the room.

"This is really a great place. Just how I pictured it

would be, Sis," he grinned. "And Weeble. I had no idea she had turned into such a super-looking lady. You were a chubby little kid when you moved out here, then a scrawny eight-year-old at my graduation, but now—you're almost fifteen, right?"

"Next month." My cheeks were on fire again. I hoped that Mom wouldn't notice. But her eyes were riveted on her brother. As I studied both of them I could see the resemblance. They had the same eyes and nose. Nicky's chin was longer, but his body had the same nervous intensity as he prowled about the room. He came back and stood in front of the sun-deck window watching a sloop buck in the cut to Newport Harbor. "This is just fabulous!"

"I can borrow a boat this weekend and take you out," Mom suggested.

"Great. I'd love it. There's so much I want to do, but first, you two. Let me take you out to dinner."

"Nope. My treat." Mom was on her feet, wagging her finger as if to remind Nicky that she was still the older sister.

"We'll discuss it on the way," he said.

Mom had her arm around my waist. I knew what was coming. She pulled me over in front of Nicky. She liked to point out to everyone that we were the same size. It assured her that she wasn't getting any older. "What do you think—pretty good shape for a thirty-two-year-old woman, huh?"

"Thirty-three," I corrected her.

"Just," she added.

He bear-hugged both of us to him. "Great. Both of you!"

I hauled out a peach-colored sundress with crisscrossing back straps that I only wore on special occasions. I noticed when I had it on that the front fit tighter and fuller than it had the last time. I thought about wearing a different one, afraid that Mom would tease me for trying to be extra feminine—an unusual event for me—but I stuck with the peach. It made me feel older.

Nicky was in Mom's office/sewing room when I came out. I remembered that Mom and I were going to clean up the room and prepare it for him that evening, but his unexpected arrival had surprised us.

"You look lovely," he said when he came into the living room.

I turned away and tried to busy myself by straightening a jumble of newspapers and magazines, embarrassed by his compliments. I wasn't used to having a man around the house, much less one who appreciated me so much. It sure was different from Mom. When she bustled out of her bedroom, she ignored me and turned her attentions on Nicky.

"Where do you want to go? There's a cozy little Italian restaurant not far. You think he'd like Pasquale's?" she asked me. Before I could answer, she went on. "Or we've got gobs of Mexican places. You like Japanese food?"

He chuckled. "Anything is fine. Just somewhere we can sit and talk, okay?" I watched him be amused by Mom's fastidiousness as she arranged a vase of dried flowers on the coffee table. She had a comical way of doing unnecessary things. Pleased with her decorating, she fastened her sandals and jumped up. "Ready?"

We agreed on a nearby Mexican restaurant that was known for its sumptuous buffets. All the way to the restaurant, Mom kept turning around as she drove to tell Nicky things. He stretched out in the back seat and attempted to look at the scenery, but every minute she was yakking at him again. I suspected he was tired and would have enjoyed a bit of silence, but when my mom gets going she doesn't notice how others are responding. She just goes.

A mariachi band greeted us at the door, and a señorita led us through a maze of tables to an intimate corner. Mom jabbered on all the while about how was Uncle Red and had Fort Wayne changed much and she hoped Nicky could stay long. I felt sorry for him.

After we were settled into our seats, I tried to get her to ease up on him. Our waitress came over. Nicky startled me when he began speaking Spanish to her. I guess I hadn't realized that people in Indiana could learn Spanish, too.

"What'd you say?" I asked him after she left.

"I told her I had come all the way from the Midwest to enjoy her food. A little flattery always makes for better service."

Mom may have been older, but Nicky had suddenly taken charge. He disguised a yawn, but Mom still picked up that he was tired. Exhausted, he corrected her. I tried not to be too obvious about staring at Nicky, but I don't think I did a good job of hiding my fascination.

Our waitress returned with three iced glasses. A lime wedge floated in each. She added a bowl of tortilla chips.

"What's this?" I asked as I pointed at the glass.

"A margarita," Nicky grinned.

I glanced over at Mom. "Don't I have to be older to drink this?"

"It's a special occasion," Nicky broke in. "I think your mother will allow you to drink this once." He arched his eyebrows and waited for her to reply.

As much as Mom drank with her friends, she had kept a strict rein on my curiosity toward adult beverages. But she winked at me and said, "Sure. We'll supervise her."

I sipped my margarita. It was tart but the salt on the rim of the glass made a pleasant contrast. They watched for my reaction. "Ummm. I think I'm hooked."

I was afraid Mom would prattle on again, but she had calmed down. Nicky explained his decision to come to the West Coast and then told about how the last band he played with had split up. I only pecked at my food when it arrived. When our waitress came back later, Nicky conversed with her in Spanish and then nodded at me.

I could have crawled under the table a couple of minutes later when she returned with a flaming cake. I blew out the candles and managed to croak, "What's the special occasion?"

He held my hand. "For all your birthdays I've missed."

Mom was happy. Her eyes were aglow as she watched Nicky across the table. It seemed strange to me that she made such a to-do when relatives came to visit, because she'd go for months without so much as sending a note, sometimes even neglecting birthdays or anniversaries. The spunk had gone out of her. She pushed away her plate and shut her eyes, listening to the mariachi band across the room serenade a tableful of old women. The women looked like they could have licked the singer's hand if he had held it out to them.

I nearly fainted when a blond, bearded giant stopped

at our table to speak with Nicky. Nicky introduced him as the drummer in Air Supply, a friend Nicky had worked with on a gig in Chicago. Air Supply was going to be performing in San Diego the next week. He invited Nicky to come down, and then asked about concert tickets for Mom and me. The drummer wrote down a telephone number on a napkin and apologized that he couldn't stay but that, because they were both on the coast, he hoped he would connect up with Nicky again.

Nicky turned back to us smiling. "The *real* Air Supply?" I asked. He nodded. I was sure I would slide onto the floor, but he explained that the music business was actually smaller than most people thought, and when you were in it long enough, you got to know about everybody. I couldn't wait to get home and call Robyn.

"Quite a coincidence, isn't it," Mom said. "You're here for a couple of hours and you've already run into someone you know."

"It's a small world."

"I guess," Mom agreed. She excused herself to visit the ladies' room.

"Can you really get tickets to the concert?" I asked after she had left. Nicky snapped his fingers. If eyes could laugh, his would have roared out loud. I saw my reflection in them. For some reason I got fluttery inside. I wasn't nervous, but the way Nicky stared at me, I was sure he had X-ray vision and could read my thoughts.

"We're going to have fun, Miss Miller," he said as if testing the sound of the words. I felt tingly all over. The mariachi band worked their way over to our table and began a slow Spanish love song. The singer must have thought I was Nicky's date, because he kept winking at Nicky. Nicky could understand what he was singing, though, and I began to get warm all over. It was partly the margarita and partly the way the band misunderstood my being there with Nicky, but by the time Mom returned, I could have been scraped off my chair with a spoon. Nicky laughed as if it was our private joke. I don't think Mom picked up on anything.

After dinner we drove to the coastal overlook on the way home. The surf pounded in as usual against the cliff rocks. A lone light out beyond the breakwaters disappeared every time a wave swelled. Probably a fisherman, I judged. I suggested we walk down to the beach, but Mom, of all people, admitted she was too tired. "There will be plenty of time for that," she sighed. The three of us walked back to the car arm in arm.

I nearly fell asleep before we got home. When we were back in the living room, Mom dug out the sheets to make up Nicky's bed. Sitting on the couch, he put his arm around me while she worked. It felt so good to have him there, with us again after so long. He was almost like a missing piece to a puzzle, like we were complete together.

Mom toddled off to bed, but when I was brushing my teeth, I heard her wander back out and begin talking quietly with Nicky. They were still talking when I tucked myself in. I dozed off with Spanish guitars and marimbas dancing in my head, and Nicky's face, like warm sunshine against mine.

Seven

Mrs. Willis droned on about hygiene. It's a course all ninth graders are required to take, even though the pictures in our book are of kids with crew cuts and women with beehives of hair—a little out of date.

Everyone watched the clock push slowly toward three o'clock. Two guys to my left had their heads down on their desks, but Mrs. Willis was unperturbed. I think we all felt a little sorry for her, or it was so late in the day that no one wanted to cause a fuss. So we sat and drowsed and waited for the final bell.

I printed my name on my notebook and festooned it with Gothic curlicues. Then I wrote *Nicky* with a wild flourish next to mine. He promised to be home after my cheerleading practice to take me with him down the coast, if he rented the car he wanted. I was anxious to show him my favorite coves and cliff formations all the way to San Juan Capistrano. It was only an hour's drive, and we could probably make it down and back before Mom rolled in.

At four minutes to three, one of the two sleeping boys toppled out of his desk and clunked to the floor. I think his head must have hurt, the way he sat up rubbing it, startled, but everyone laughed. By the time Mrs. Willis got our attention again, the bell rang. As I filed into the noisy hallway, I searched for Robyn. We were to meet by my locker for cheerleading practice.

While I waited, a super cute guy I didn't know stopped to ask me for change.

"Isn't he a fox!" Robyn crooned in my ear after I had given him two dimes and a nickel and he had moved on. "He sits right next to me in English class. I think I'm in love." She rolled her eyes back like a delirious cow. Speechless, I jammed the junk from my purse back in, scooped up my workout bag, and headed down the hall. "Hey, wait up a sec," Robyn called.

She caught me at the gym entrance. "Why are you so huffy?"

"No reason," I answered sharply. "Let's get dressed. I want to punish my body today after all I ate last night."

"Oh yeah? You didn't tell me much at lunch. When do I get to meet this uncle? And when can I hear him sing, huh? Are you going to be a friend and share him with me, or keep him all for yourself."

"Will you get serious," I said. "He's my uncle, okay? My mom's brother. And he's almost ten years older than you."

"So is Rick Springfield," she grinned. "And I wouldn't complain, not a bit. Oh, I forgot my socks."

"You can borrow my extra pair," I said. "In fact, they're new. I haven't even worn them yet." I tossed her the new socks. She unrolled them and put them to her nose.

"Ummm, new socks always smell so good."

"Just wear them, don't eat them," I said.

Mrs. Williams came out of her office to announce that tryouts were about to start and all valuables should be turned over to her for safekeeping right away. I followed Robyn into the drafty gym and went through the motions of warming up.

My head seemed fuzzy and I had trouble getting started. Robyn noticed my sluggishness.

"I thought you were going to be harsh on yourself?"

"I'm so stiff," I moaned. "Maybe I need my ten-thousand-mile checkup."

"Not me," she said between twists. "I jogged at six this morning and I feel tremendous."

I didn't know if she was teasing. The determination on her face said she wasn't. "Really? You're going all out to get in shape for tryouts, aren't you?"

She began doing knee bends, almost ferociously. I had never seen her so intent on physical exercise, but she kept on, struggling until perspiration beaded her forehead. I felt like a lazy slob watching her. My heart wasn't in the routine exercises I found boring and repetitive. I preferred handsprings and solo leaps, the springs that required agility. Plodding through warm-ups was not for me.

Mrs. Williams called for attention. "You may work individually or in small groups," she said, "but don't anyone leave without my permission. Now go to work."

Robyn and I teamed up with Sissy and Autumn, two friends from grade school. Sissy towered above our group and Autumn was pudgier than Robyn, but when we rehearsed in unison, I doubt if any group yelled louder. By the time we broke for water, our movements had become fairly coordinated.

I hung over the fountain and drank in the icy water. Behind me in line, Jennifer, with her usual retinue, made a snide remark about Mr. Blair. I caught just the last part of it.

"What was that?" I wiped my mouth.

"You heard me," she replied. She folded her arms and pretended to look away. I felt my ears redden.

"No, I didn't." She ignored me. I had bottled a lot of anger toward her because of the drugstore incident, and now I felt it surging up. I went over and stood in front of her. She couldn't ignore me. A phony smile, effortless, I thought. She kept her pasted-on smile and told me to drop it.

"I won't," I said. "Not unless you repeat what you said."

A sigh, as if to tell me Why bother? But she realized that I wasn't going to back off. "I said, that you probably had cheerleading cinched again because of Mr. Blair."

"And what does that mean?"

"He's a judge, isn't he?" She smiled at a friend.

"So?"

"So, you're his little darling, aren't you? I even heard that you slept with him last year to make it."

I felt myself losing control as I stared into her vacant eyes. A smudge of eye shadow was on her upper cheek. I thought momentarily of raking five fingernails across the spot, but Robyn tugged at my arm. Everyone was waiting for my reaction. "That is a lie," I hissed. "A sick disgusting lie, and I do not wish to hear you ever say it again. Ever. Understand?" She glanced away. Her friends tittered, unsure what I was going to do. I fought down the revulsion that wanted to see her pretty face crack apart. I wanted her to shrivel and be plain, be ugly like the rest of us, but she stood defiantly. Mrs. Williams pushed through the group that had crowded around.

"Not another fight," she said tiredly. "It's either the weather or a full moon, but something's gotten into you girls. Let's go back to work. The boys have the gym soon. Let's go everybody," she said clapping her hands.

Everyone scattered back to their groups. I watched Jennifer flounce over to her friends, as if she had proved her point. No one believed what she had said about me and Mr. Blair, but she had said it and gotten away with it. It was outrageous and untrue—still, to say it was to put doubts in everyone's heads when the time came for the final judging. All who had heard her would watch Mr. Blair for his reaction when I began my cheers.

"What a slime," Robyn spit. "I'd like to make mashed potatoes of her face." Robyn always said things like that when she was sure no one could hear. "Mr. Blair," she said horrified.

I remembered that not too long ago she confessed to me a dream she'd had about Mr. Blair. It was a good seven point five on the blush scale, but that didn't seem to revolt her like Jennifer's insinuation. Frankly, I didn't see much difference. Mr. Blair *was* the most eligible teacher at Oceanside; because he was young and handsome may have accounted for his large following of female students. Still, he was my mom's age.

For the rest of cheerleading I wondered what Nicky was up to. He promised he would find a convertible. He even hinted that he might take me to the parking lot and teach me to drive. I was old enough for my learner's permit, even though I had never expressed much interest about it to my mother.

When our foursome split up to head home, we felt proud of what we had accomplished. Robyn, in particular, remarked that no other group had our precision.

"Have you lost weight?" Autumn asked Robyn. Leave it to her to notice weight.

I could tell Robyn was pleased. "Already six pounds," she grinned. "I want to make cheerleading real bad."

"Me too," Autumn said. "But I doubt if I will."

I headed home. The late sun on the parking-lot pavement was hot. It made the tar gooey. I liked being barefoot, even though the bottoms of my feet were almost permanently black. I stopped to wait for Robyn at the corner. She ran up shaking her head. "Some people will do anything for attention."

"Like who?"

"Well, I was thinking of Jennifer. That was rotten for her to say what she did. Especially since we didn't make a big deal about her shoplifting."

"Come on," I said over my shoulder. "I've got to hurry home and shower so I can go for a ride with Nicky."

"Doesn't what she said bother you though?" She caught my stride.

65

"I think it bothers you more. Besides"—I kept a straight face—"it might be true."

She looked startled, then her face relaxed. "No, seriously. I'm not going to forget what she said."

We hurried across a busy street. "Who cares?"

"I do." She glanced over at me. "Somebody has to."

Just as we hopped onto the curb, a powder blue convertible, an import, pulled alongside us honking. "Want a ride?" Nicky grinned. He held the door open for us. I slid in and glanced up at Robyn. She stared, mouth open, her droopy eyes big, as if to say, Wow! For real?

She finally snapped out of her trance. "Get in"—I smiled—"and meet Nicky."

"I'm uh . . ." It was the first time I had ever heard her stutter.

"I know, you're Robyn," Nicky said as we sped away.

I felt her turn to jelly next to me.

Eight

I was in the middle of a great dream when I sensed someone looming over me. It took a moment to determine if I had just awakened in my dream or if I was really awake. A shadow moved across my bed. I squinted up, and then I realized someone was in the room pawing through my top dresser drawer.

I froze, expecting at any instant to feel a knife driven through my chest, or worse, to be suffocated by one of my own socks if I so much as squeaked. Pretending I was still asleep seemed like the best strategy. With my heart thumping like a dynamo, I tried to listen to the intruder's movements. The figure shut the drawer and approached my bed.

A cold hand touched my forearm. I shrieked.

"Sssssshh. Weeble. It's just me." I recognized Robyn's voice. She knelt down next to the bed. "I didn't want to wake you."

"God, I about died of fright," I murmured. A slice of light from the streetlamp illuminated one side of her face. She looked exhausted. "What time is it? What are you doing here?" I leaned on one elbow.

"I really didn't want to sneak in," she apologized. "I used the key you leave under your doormat. I hope you don't mind."

I tried to clear my head. The sudden fear had left my thoughts buzzing like night bugs. She slumped against the bed wearily. "What is going on, Robyn?"

"I'm running away," she sighed. "I was going to borrow some of your clothes since I didn't have time to pack."

"What?" I peered down at her tear-streaked face. "You've been crying. Something happened at home again, didn't it?" She nodded. "Your parents have a fight?" Again right. "A big one?"

"Fifteen rounds," she said softly. "I was sleeping when my dad came home, pretty late I think. My mom started screaming like she was being killed, so I rushed out and saw that she was only drunk. But furious, you know. She was circling him like a cobra, and he just kept shaking his head and telling her to calm down because she was upsetting me."

She shook her head and lay next to me. I stroked her brow. I didn't know what to tell her. I wanted to understand what made her parents the way they were, why they had to fight and not get anything solved, but I couldn't. Nothing made sense. I picked up my watch from the bedside table and studied it. "It's three-twenty," I whispered.

"I really didn't want to wake you. I just wanted to get some clothes and go."

"Go where?" She shrugged and closed her eyes. I tried to smooth her wrinkled forehead. She was still visibly upset.

She began brokenly. "I just . . . can't take it anymore. Got to get away . . . you know . . . glue my head back together." She sniffed, her whole body tense against my hand.

"I don't want to sound like your mother, but running away is no solution. You'll just make everything worse." Her shoulders began to shake, and then her whole body trembled, racked in agony.

"Oh God, Weeble, I just don't know what to do. I can't talk to them. I thought maybe if I just vanish for a while then maybe . . . maybe . . . I don't know."

I slid past her and crept over to my closet, trying not to disturb my mother, who was a light sleeper. I hauled out the sleeping bag and unrolled it next to my bed. Without protest, she stretched out on it, shuddering faintly. There was nothing I could think of to soothe her. Perhaps my mother would have an idea in the morning.

"I don't want to get you involved, Weeble. It's not fair to you."

"Just relax, okay? The important thing is that you don't run away. I'd hate to see anything worse happen to you. We'll figure everything out later. Can you sleep?"

"I don't think so. My stomach is still churning."

I went into the kitchen to see if we had any Seven Up. Mom's door was cracked just slightly, but I couldn't hear her. I hoped she was out soundly. Nicky's door was shut tight.

When I handed Robyn the bottle she took a long swallow and began to choke. I thumped her on the back until she stopped. "Went down the wrong way," she explained.

"Do your parents know you left?"

She took a sip and shook her head. "Unh-uh. They could care less. I think my dad is going to move out soon."

"Why?"

"I don't think he's going to put up with Mom much longer. He's changed so much. He hardly talks to me anymore. And he is never goofy or relaxed the way he used to be. In the last couple of months things have gotten really bad."

I thought back to when I first met Robyn's parents. Her father always had a silly, mischievous grin when I was around. Sometimes he would tease us until we'd turn red with laughter. And he always had a joke to tell us, usually one that elicited groans.

"But my mom is the one I'm really worried about," she continued. With the color gone from her face she looked pale and ghostly. "When she's been moping around all day, going through bottle after bottle, she can hardly talk at night. She slurs her words, you know." She demonstrated. "I think she even stopped eating. She used to be so pretty, but she's letting herself go, and she won't see a doctor or a counselor and all she does is yell, even at me, for no reason. I gotta get out of there or I'm going to crack up. That's why I thought if I disappeared, then maybe they would get worried and snap out of the way they're acting for a while, you know? Maybe they'd get scared, get sober long enough to see what's happening to our family."

I thought over what she said. Children were powerless to change their parents, that was obvious. Running away might affect them for a short time, but the serious problems would remain. If anything, Robyn would appear less mature, even unstable. I didn't want to think of the possibilities if she was successful in running away. Occasionally I saw the results of teenage runaways along the beach; the kids looked so sad, so burnt out. The girl's faces were hard, creased with heavy makeup. The guys drifted into trouble.

If Robyn was too distraught to think clearly, I had to take care of her. We had to protect each other. Our parents may have been responsible for bringing us into the world, but now Robyn and I had to fend for ourselves. We had to see that nothing happened. My mother would understand.

"Robyn," I tried to find the words. "You know, you're pretty important to me. I don't have any brothers or sisters, and, well . . . you know. . . ."

She took my hand and squeezed it. "I do."

"And you can stay as long as you want."

"I know." She closed her eyes. I sat listening to her. Her breathing gradually slowed until I knew she was asleep. I put my head down on my arm and tried to recall what my unfinished dream had been about. I finally managed to get back into it, but then Mom was shaking me awake.

I felt like an unmade bed as I stomped into the bathroom. There was no time for a shower. Robyn was trying to pull on a pair of my jeans when I came back. Frustrated, she gave up and stared at me from the floor with the jeans stuck midway along her hips. I went to borrow a pair of my mother's for her.

"Is Nicky up?" she asked me shyly.

"Are you kidding? Maybe by noon."

Mom didn't say anything about Robyn sleeping over when we came into the kitchen. She sat at the table stirring her coffee.

"You two better hurry!"

I glanced up at the clock. "We'll grab something on the way to school to eat."

"No you won't. Knowing you, it would be a doughnut. I've got fresh peaches in the refrigerator. Grab one to eat on the way." She usually bustled about late herself, but I think she was lingering to see we got safely on our way.

As we went out the door, she seemed to remember something. "You might be interested in knowing I got a call from one of your teachers last night." A half dozen faces flashed through my head. I couldn't think of who I had offended. "A certain Mr. Blair," she smiled. "Next Friday, for dinner."

I tried to contain my squeals as I pushed Robyn out the door.

"Are you trying to bribe him for cheerleading?" She laughed.

Nine

The whirlwind of following days was incredible. Between school and cheerleading practice and tour-guiding Nicky here and there, it seemed my mom was trying to compress a year of activities into a week.

She let me stay home from school one day and even took a personal-leave day herself—a rare occurrence—so we could take Nicky to the Huntington Beach Amusement Park. "We'll have it all to ourselves," she rationalized, "if we go on a weekday."

And so we did. There was none of the long, weekend lines. We hardly waited for anything. Though Mom refused to go on the Tidal Wave, a gigantic snaking roller coaster, Nicky went with me five times. Before the final run he coaxed me into the front car, and as we started the long climb to the top of the first drop, he turned to me, a childish delight in his eyes, and said, "I'll hold my arms up if you will."

"I'll fall out if I don't hold on," I said. But I knew I wouldn't, because half the people who rode the Tidal Wave usually held their arms up without grabbing the safety bar. I was worried about the middle though, where the cars made a complete upside-down revolution.

"No," Nicky said, encouraging me, "centrifugal force will hold you in. Come on—go for it!"

I was scared to death, but as we approached the crest, Nicky lifted his arms above his head and I did the same. I was going to grab tight when I got my first glimpse of the ground a couple hundred feet below, but we shot back down so fast I couldn't pull my arms in.

When we hit the center loop I thought for sure I would drop out and be killed, but Nicky was right, I stuck to my seat. I did scream all the way until we finally rolled to the loading platform. I squeezed Nicky's arm with a feeling of accomplishment. Never before had I been as brave; Nicky helped me prove to myself that I wasn't a kid anymore.

My mom, sucking a cherry snowcone at a nearby bench, merely shook her head. "You two are crazy," she said between slurps.

"I can't wait to tell Robyn," I said.

We decided on hot dogs for lunch, but my stomach was a bit queasy, so I just nibbled at mine and listened to Mom and Nicky. They rambled on mostly about relatives back in the Midwest, most of whom I remembered only vaguely.

"And does Mom still bake the best sourdough bread in the country?" my mom asked.

"And you remember Richard, the little old man at the drugstore," Nicky was saying, but I only picked up snatches of what they said as I pored over the amusement-park map, plotting out the direction we would go next.

We had to go on the log ride again, then the bumper cars, the Ferris wheel, and of course, the haunted house. Mom liked the House of Mirrors, and I wanted the parachute drop, but that was another ride my mom would avoid.

They would have gone on yakking all afternoon if I hadn't hauled them off the bench.

"But Mom," I pleaded, "we haven't gone on half the rides."

Nicky laughed at my eagerness and put his arm around my mom. I liked to see such affection between them, and it made us feel almost like a perfect family if he had been my father. But I dismissed the thought as soon as it surfaced. I loved Nicky, but he could never replace a real father.

"Weeble, what about the Super Screamer?" Nicky grabbed my hand and pointed to a whiplash special that flung people at one another, then snapped them back in opposite directions, as the cars caromed past in near collisions.

"Pass," I groaned. "My lunch hasn't even hit my stomach yet."

"Okay, later," he said.

We all agreed to climb aboard the miniature tootle train that circled the amusement park then skirted the boardwalk and beach front. A brisk ocean wind made me scoot closer to Nicky; Mom, in the seat across from us, smiled and zipped up her windbreaker.

I detected something different about her, a contentment the past few days. She was more at peace with herself, pleased, I think, that Nicky had opened a direct channel to her past. Usually she was too busy to talk about her childhood, a subject totally fascinating to me, but with Nicky she was open and relaxed. I liked to see that in her. Nicky was having a positive influence on both of us.

After the train ride, we went into the bumper-car track. We were the only ones riding, and as we chased each other about, the weirdest thought came to me. I had smashed into people lots of times before, even Robyn, when we'd ridden the bumper cars. But every time I had the opportunity to crash my mom or Nicky, I eased off. A couple times I swerved out of the way to avoid them altogether. Nicky sideswiped me once, and Mom rammed me good and drove me against the rail, but I tried hard not to hit them.

After the bumper cars we climbed on the carousel. My horse, a wildly plunging palomino, raced Nicky's horse around and around in ever faster circles. I threw my head back as the colors and smells and sounds merged into the speed of the revolving horses. I glanced over my shoulder at my mother who sprawled back in a carriage being drawn by two sea horses.

After that I lost track of what we rode on next. I do recall how I felt when Mom and Nicky beat me into the two-person car at the Pirates Cove and I got stuck riding alone. It upset me to ride by myself without anyone to grab a hold of when the pirates swooped down out of the darkness.

The time was gone before my energy ran out. Nicky

bought me a cuddly brown monkey as a souvenir, and as we piled into Mom's car he gave her a key chain with a huge whistle on it. I couldn't stop yawning on the way home, even though it was only late afternoon.

I showered and then I called Robyn, but she was at her orthodontist's. After spending the night at her house, she had decided that running away wasn't the answer.

Mom suggested we drive down to Balboa Island, catch the ferry across to the peninsula and have dinner at one of the seafood restaurants. We did and it capped a day for the record books. Not once had my mom talked about work.

The lights on bobbing sailboats gleamed about us as we chugged across the dark bay to the pavilion. I loved to hear the ferry whistle. In the middle, the ferryman shut down his engine and coasted toward the other dock. The harbor was nearly deserted. The cool, salt-scented breeze ruffled my hair, and the waves' *slap-slap* was the only sound as we drifted to the mooring post. A girl with a bicycle waited at the dock.

"Gosh, this is so beautiful," Nicky said. Sometimes he acted like a kid, overcome by the beauty of life. This was one of those times.

We kicked off our shoes when we got to the beach. The sand still held some of the day's heat, but the closer we got to the water, the cooler the sand became. Soft breakers pushed driftwood up the beach. A pile of seaweed swished in and out.

"Why would anyone want to live in the cold Midwest when they could have this?" my mom remarked.

"Really," Nicky added.

No one said much after that. I doubt if my mom was talked out, but the sky was soon ablaze with stars against the horizon. The waves swashed continually upon the hard-packed sand, and we walked in silence. When we reached the pier we put on our shoes.

After dinner we watched a solitary fisherman at the pier's end smoking in the dark and staring out to sea. As we turned back toward the harbor and the ferry that would take us back to our car, Nicky asked Mom softly if she ever missed home.

"No, this is my home now," she said. And then we were all quiet.

On Saturday we were hot and sticky by mid-morning. Deciding on the beach was easy enough. We loaded a cooler, blankets, Frisbee, suntan lotion, a radio, and beach towels. Mom always made it a regular expedition, but I didn't complain. I was too worried about which suit to wear—my too-tight, one-piece with the bright geometric stripes, or my yellow bikini. I chose the bikini, even though the suntan marks from my one-piece were still visible.

I thought of calling Robyn to ask her along, but we seemed in so much of a hurry that I just couldn't. Besides, I told myself, she would be too self-conscious about wearing a bathing suit in front of Nicky.

We went to Corona Del Mar, where we could watch the sailboats passing through the cut to open sea. The beach was already crowded. We selected an open area near a volleyball game to set up camp. Nicky didn't have swim trunks, but he had some cutoffs. At times like this

I was struck suddenly again by how good-looking he was. I was a little shy about rubbing lotion on his back, but he didn't notice. Mom settled back on her blanket and opened a thick paperback novel to the middle and started reading.

She got bored easily at the beach. While I could just watch the stream of people, she needed something to occupy her time. Nicky was like me. He leaned back on his elbows to check out the beach crowd.

Two of the guys in the volleyball game were from my school. One of them was gorgeous, tall, tanned, and blond, and once somebody told me he thought I was cute, but he never called and that was that. I liked how he jumped high at the net to spike a return shot. He grinned and shook his hair back. He was too engrossed in the game to notice us.

Two college girls strolled past our blanket. It was interesting to watch Nicky's reaction. His head swiveled slowly after them and he sighed to himself. It was the first time I'd seen him act like a normal adult male, and it shouldn't have surprised me, but it did.

I don't know what I expected. Mom was lost in her book. Nicky, from time to time, would glance to his right at three girls on a blanket not far away. One was lying on her stomach. She had untied the strap to the top of her suit. Her back glistened. I tried to imagine what Nicky was thinking as he stared at her naked back for a long time.

It was hard to define what I thought, but when the girl sat up to turn over, she held her top to her chest, exposing one of her breasts. Nicky whistled softly, but the girl was oblivious to everything. She adjusted her position and lay back down.

For a second I felt a little angry, not at Nicky, but at her, though I still didn't know why. Maybe just the natural protective instincts of the female species, I said to myself.

I closed my eyes and sank back onto the warm sand. I started to drift off until Nicky kissed me lightly on the forehead and I opened one eye. "Want something cold to drink, Sleeping Beauty?" I shook my head, then sat back up to people-watch some more.

A young couple ambled past, arm in arm. They could have stepped off the pages of *Seventeen Magazine*'s summer issue, they were so perfect looking. It almost gagged me to see them, so I plopped back down and tried to doze in the sun. It wasn't like me to be depressed by the "competition," as Robyn would say, yet I was. Mom's page turning and Nicky's occasional sighs and the blanket of warm, enveloping sun lulled me into half-consciousness.

I hadn't realized Nicky was gone until I felt his absence, like a presence in itself. Mom was still thumbing her book with oily fingers and the volleyball game was into its second hour, but Nicky was not in sight.

"Where's Nicky?"

"Took a walk," my mom answered. She dug into the cooler for a can of pop. "Want a root beer?" I shook my head. "Ice cold."

"No thanks."

"It's low calorie."

"Unh-uh. I'm not thirsty." I scanned the beach in both directions, but I didn't see Nicky. The three girls on the blanket near us were still sprawled out. I couldn't go off in search of him because I'd feel dumb walking by myself, but I couldn't go with my mother—not that I don't love her—but that wouldn't be neat either. I wished he had asked me to go with him.

After a bit I saw him climbing along the rocks on the point. He turned back after scrambling over a large boulder to help a girl with long brown hair. Her hair was easily to her waist. He didn't turn toward her again until they reached the dunes at the end of the point, then she came up and stood next to him and pointed out at a sailboat, as if explaining something. I resented her, even though I didn't know her and didn't know how Nicky knew her.

But I didn't rule his life, so it wasn't for me to say to whom he could and couldn't talk. I didn't like it though, and I knew it was childish of me to think that way, but I couldn't help it.

Mom was back in her book, so I didn't say anything. After a while I tried to ignore Nicky and the girl, but my curiosity kept winning. They didn't touch and they only looked at each other a couple of times, but there was a male-female communication passing between them. It bothered me and I felt guilty about being mad. It got too confusing for me to think about, so I shut my eyes, tilted my face back toward the sun, and tried to force out any thought that floated up from my mind. It worked after a bit.

When I next opened my eyes, Nicky and the girl were gone. A couple of minutes later he came back by himself and didn't volunteer any information. We flipped the Frisbee back and forth until I missed a catch and kicked sand all over a fat guy's picnic basket. He was understanding, but I didn't want to make a fool of myself any longer, so we returned to our blankets.

Mom was three hundred pages into the book and unaware of how much time had passed, but Nicky's shoulders were starting to cook, and rather than let them get any redder, we decided to head home.

Nicky went to use the shower first and Mom took the towels down to the laundry room. Feeling restless, I trudged after her.

"Hey Pumpkin, got any homework this weekend?" She didn't act surprised to see me. I watched her set the controls. She hadn't punched on the hot-water button, so I did. She didn't say anything.

"No, not really. Just a book report."

"So, how's Robyn doing?"

"I don't know. I have to call her."

"What's up? You seem kind of quiet. Anything wrong?" She felt my forehead out of habit, but I wasn't sick.

"Oh, I don't know—nothing really. It's just kind of nice having a man around the house, isn't it?"

"Of course it is, but aren't I a good enough mother?"

"I didn't mean that."

She bent over to brush some sand off her legs. When she stood back up she looked at me carefully. There were white circles around her eyes from her sunglasses. "Of course I like having a man around, but that doesn't mean that I'm going to find one to replace Nicky when he leaves."

"Wouldn't you like to have him stay though?"

"He can stay as long as he wants, but he's got plans,

and who knows what may happen with his career? We've done pretty well for ourselves up until now and I think we can manage just fine—with or without a man around."

"But don't you ever imagine what it might be like if you had a husband and I had a father?"

"Well, Roger has asked me a half dozen times to marry him."

"Don't make me gag, Mom. We're not desperate."

"We're? You talk like this is a joint decision. What if I did decide to marry Roger? He has a good job, he likes you and could give us both security."

"Those aren't reasons to get married."

"So now you're the expert?" She added her whose-the-mother-whose-the-daughter smile. Sometimes, and she knew it, I did feel like I was the mother and she my daughter. This wasn't one, though.

"I just mean that our house feels more complete with a woman *and* a man in it. Not a storybook family, but—I don't know. I can't explain it."

"Babe," she said, patting my hand. "I know what you're trying to say. If the right man comes along, we'll marry him, okay? For now, we'll enjoy Nicky while we have him."

She sighed in a knowing-mother way and put her arm around me as we walked back to the apartment.

I wasn't sure I could ever share her with a man after everything we'd been through. Nicky wasn't threatening of her attentions, but why had I been jealous to see him acting normal toward other women at the beach? No, it wasn't jealousy, I convinced myself. It was something else, but I didn't have a name for it.

Ten

On Monday, on the way home from school, I heard Nicky strumming his guitar a block away from our building. As I drew closer, I recognized the tune as one from the Eagles; it sounded like "Hotel California." I skipped up the steps, dropped my schoolbooks just inside the door, and plopped down in front of him on the floor. He had his eyes closed and didn't even know I was home.

He played well. I watched his hands slide expertly over the strings, all the while his head rocked rhythmically from side to side. Finally, he hung on the final chord and then paused. His eyes slowly opened.

"Whoa! When did you sneak in?" he exclaimed. He sat forward, his eyes sparkly like a Fourth of July twilight.

"A few minutes ago. I didn't want to disturb you. You looked like you were in a world of your own."

"I was." He grinned. "I always am when I get into the music. It just sweeps me away. I can almost see the melody line spinning off my guitar like gigantic colored swirls, or clouds of . . . feeling, you know?"

"I don't, but it sure sounds neat. I wish I could play something."

He chuckled and sat back plunking a funny tune. He could make his guitar sound like a lovesick bullfrog. "How's school?" he asked when he stopped.

"Ugh! The same. A couple of weeks and then I'm free for the summer."

"And then what?"

"I don't know. Goof around, I guess."

"Uh-huh." He edged off the sofa and settled cross-legged onto the floor. He stuck a bare foot against mine. It tickled, but I didn't pull away. "This is for you." His easy smile went clean through me. I studied his thin, muscular hands as the guitar began to speak again. It made me think of a language, the way the gentle sounds flowed about us in the air. Earlier, the language was harsh and angry. Now, it was whispering, crooning like wind in the eucalyptus trees, like waves across undisturbed sand. I closed my eyes and felt the warmth all about me. Everything seemed to come from Nicky's hands, like magic. I opened one eye, and the light was dazzling, emanating from the sun glow reflected off the guitar.

When he stopped, I went on swaying for a minute. He had almost lulled me to sleep.

"Ummm," I sighed. "That was nice. Whose song is it?"

"Mine," he said. "I wrote it. But I give it to you if you like it."

"Really?"

"Sure. I hadn't given it a title yet, but now it's called 'Elizabeth's Song.' It sounds better than Weeble."

I didn't argue. It was the first song ever named just for me, and it was beautiful. I was flattered. He scooted closer to me, and his legs brushed mine.

He was so relaxed and comfortable that I found it difficult to imagine the skinny, overactive teenager I barely remembered from Indiana. He scrutinized my face until I had to turn away embarrassed. "You sure have grown up, young lady, but you've still got a cute little nose," he said. "It reminds me of a pixie."

"A pixie?" I giggled.

"Yeah, like the blue fairy. Kind of a Tinkerbell nose. Dainty. It fits your face."

"I hope so." I blushed. I looked up at him. Tiny smile wrinkles wove into the corners of his eyes. With some people you meet for the first time, you just can tell they're happy people from the contours of their faces, the way their lines all point up into a smile. Nicky's face was like that. He seemed to be smiling even when he wasn't.

"Nicky?" I said, hesitating.

"Yes, Blue Fairy?"

"No, now cut that out." I grinned and punched him playfully on the arm.

"What?" he asked softly.

"Tell me about my father."

"Hmmmmm . . . your father." He sighed and leaned back on his elbows. He seemed thoughtful, almost like he was hesitant to tell me something.

"What was he like? Mom never tells me anything, like it's something she wants to keep buried."

"What's passed is past."

"That's what she always says, too. But I want to know. After all, he was *my* father. I'm entitled to know something about him, aren't I?" I didn't want to plead with him, but perhaps he could color in some details of the unfinished picture in my mind.

"Well . . . I don't remember too much."

"Anything."

"He was tall . . . of course, I was only about ten years old, so any adult seemed tall to me."

"What else?" I studied his face as his eyes stared off into the distance.

"He always smelled good, like a strong and clean aftershave." He flipped the memory pages while my heart began to pound wildly. "And he had big hands, because he would always swing me into the air—I remember that. He never came around too much. I don't think our parents were too crazy about him, but Sis—your mom—she sure flipped out over him."

"Is that all?"

"I guess so. To tell you the truth, Weeble, Kathy was pretty popular with the guys. I don't want to get him mixed up with somebody else. And like I said, I didn't pay much attention to things like boyfriends, since I was into tree houses and roaming the countryside and my go-cart. I wish I could tell you more."

"Me too," I sighed.

"But I'm sure your mother will tell you more someday. She probably has her reasons."

"Yeah, maybe. It's just . . ." I looked at him for reassurance. The blue of his eyes held me lovingly. "I don't know. It's too hard to explain."

87

"What, Little Blue Fairy? What?" He put his hand over mine.

"It's . . . I don't know . . . kind of an empty feeling, I guess. Like there's a hole inside me, something missing. Does that make any sense?"

"Sure." His other hand settled to the back of my neck. My weak spot. Whenever my mother had to massage my tension away, it was always the nape of my neck that sent goose bumps along my spine. He smoothed the downy hairs where they tapered between my shoulders. I was becoming like soft putty. He knew it.

"I love my mom and she's tried to be both mother and father to me. We've been through some hard times together. But . . ."

"But what?"

"But I have this need to know more. If I only knew where my father was I could write him a letter or call him or just know that he was alive and somewhere, and maybe someday I could meet him. He wouldn't have to say anything, in fact, he wouldn't even have to know it was his daughter. I'd just want to see him once to know what he looks like."

"Sorry I can't help you much," he said, still stroking my neck.

"I used to have this fantasy that I'd come across a letter from him to my mother and I found the return address, so one weekend I travel to where he lives and disguise myself like a girl scout or a door-to-door salesman, and he opens the door and is real friendly and invites me in for a cookie and cocoa, and then he sees something special in my eyes and out of the blue confides in me that he sometimes dreams of having a daughter, but you see, he doesn't know that he already has one because he moved away before I was born and he lost touch and . . ." I started to sniffle, feeling foolish at what I'd told Nicky.

He bent down and kissed me on the cheek. I took a deep breath and leaned back into his warm hand on my neck.

"Feel good?"

"Ummmmm. You've found my controls."

"That's good," he smiled. "I like to make people feel good."

I looked up at him, entranced by his eyes. I couldn't turn away and suddenly felt shivery. His face, just inches away from mine, fascinated me. I saw the kiss coming, but I couldn't turn away to avoid it. I didn't want to.

His lips on mine felt warm and spongy. He tasted clean and so fresh, as if he had just stepped out of a rain shower. Then he kissed my nose. "Blue fairy nose," he whispered. When he sat back and waited for my reaction, I felt my stomach cartwheel.

One part of me was snuggling into Nicky's warmth, but the skittery part of me inside was saying, No, this is your uncle, he's not a boyfriend, he's not your age, you shouldn't be wrapped here in his arms. But it was easy to pretend, as I stared into his eyes, that everything was all right. Nicky *was* a loving person. I hadn't seen him in so long. He was the closest male in my life now. . . .

The spicy cinnamon taste of his lips stayed on mine. I didn't resist his kiss, though I hadn't wanted to be obvious about kissing back, in case Nicky should get the wrong idea about me.

I had kissed boys before—that was no big deal. But usually we were both so nervous that it was a painful agony until our lips collided. Then, instead of feeling better about the person, I just wanted to get on with the party or wherever we were and forgo the awkward maneuvering.

With Nicky it was something different. Maybe because we had the same Miller blood or my mom between us in a special way. Maybe it was just Nicky who put me at ease, who loved me like a little sister. All of a sudden he didn't seem so old. He traced his finger around my face.

"You are like a precious, porcelain doll, so innocent, so delicate." He kissed me on the lips again, then a second and third time. I had never felt so strange before, as if my blood was singing inside me. He hugged me to him, still kissing. I think I was kissing him, too, but I wasn't quite sure what my head was saying. My body was all on its own, pressing against Nicky, my heart and his beating just inches apart.

We sort of tipped sideways, but Nicky supported both of us. For a moment, I wondered what Mom would say if she were to walk in, but I didn't care. Nicky's music was inside my mouth now, lifting my head off my shoulders.

I sat up abruptly when his hand brushed against my breast. It wasn't right. The situation there on the floor finally clicked inside me. My thoughts tumbled about, my body stiffened. What am I doing, I wondered?

Nicky sat watching me, his eyes calm, his face mellow.

I thought momentarily of easing back into his arms, but my sense had returned. It was wrong to be passionate with him, wasn't it? I did love him, and I knew he loved me, but still, it wasn't right. Thoughts raced through my mind.

I excused myself and ran into the bathroom. After I had locked the door, I sat on the side of the bathtub and began to tremble. I remembered how Robyn had shivered all over a few nights before, and now, I couldn't stop, either. I didn't want Nicky to stop loving me, but I was confused. I had never been so intimate with a man before, so close to letting a part of me I didn't understand run away like it had. I took a half dozen deep breaths and then looked at myself in the mirror. My chin was red where Nicky's beard had roughed the skin. My cheeks were flushed, but otherwise, it was the same old Weeble. Except, the ache inside had wedged its way out again. Was this what being in love meant, I wondered? My head felt so far away from my body.

I tried to think of what I would say when I came out, but all the words jumbled together like nonsense. When I returned to the living room, though, Nicky was gone. He had left me a note under the strings of his guitar. It read,

Weeble, I hope I didn't upset you. Don't get the wrong idea about me. I do love you and your mom. We'll talk more later, OK? Nicky

I felt a little better after reading that. But still, I was afraid that something I did triggered Nicky's behavior. I tried to think back, but nothing fit together. I wanted to talk to Robyn. I just wanted to hear her voice so I would know my feet were on earth again.

Her voice seemed to come from light-years away, even though her house was only a half mile down the hillside.

"Can you believe I just biked down to Laguna and back?" she said. "Eight miles round trip in under an hour. Pretty good, huh?"

"Yeah, I'm impressed."

"Hey, how's Nicky?"

I wanted to spill out the mixed-up feelings that were whirling about inside me, but all I could say was, "Fine. He's not home now though."

"Boy," Robyn said. "He is *so* neat. Goll, you're lucky. All my uncles are about fifty years old and fat and smoke cigars and get food on their moustaches. I have a cousin in San Francisco who used to be cute, but I guess he got weird, because nobody talks about him now. When I was little I went bonkers over him."

I stared out the window, only half listening to Robyn. The ocean was nearly green, like cat's-eye. The air, exceptionally clear, had no trace of smog, and the tip of Catalina Island rose against the horizon. All these years living within sight of Catalina, and I had never been there.

"You want to maybe come over for a while tonight?" Robyn's voice broke through the fog. "Nobody is going to be home. I'll make you a protein shake."

"What about your diet?"

"It's low-cal. Want to? I'll turn the heater on in the pool and we can swim. Mom doesn't like me to heat the pool, but, like I said, she'll be gone. We can pace each other laps. Lose a pound an hour by swimming. Okay?"

"Sure," I agreed. "Maybe I could—" I didn't know how to tell Robyn about what had happened with Nicky. I couldn't keep it from her. She was my best friend. But would she understand?

"What?" I knew she sensed something was wrong because of the silence. I couldn't bring it up. Not yet.

"Nothing. I was just thinking about something. I'll be over in a bit, all right?" When I hung up I thought of waiting until Mom arrived home to tell her I was spending the night with Robyn. I decided to leave her a note instead. I needed time to think. Maybe Robyn would understand.

As I went out the door I wondered if I was making everything worse than it was. Should I just forget and keep quiet? Nicky's car was in the drive, so he must have been walking. As strongly as I felt about him, I hoped I wouldn't see him. At least not until I had everything all straightened out.

Eleven

When I got to Robyn's house, I thought she might have left. There were no lights on, and she didn't answer my knocks at first. Finally, I heard her call from an upstairs window to come around through the back door and let myself in.

"Why so secret?" I asked as I met her on the stairs.

"You won't believe this," she said with a straight face, "but I think Dad has hired a detective to watch the house."

"You're kidding. What for?"

"God, it's a mess," she continued as I followed her up to her room. "I don't know for sure myself, but I think it has something to do with what I found out today."

I sat on her bed as she fished through the dresser for her swimming suit. The normal clutter I had come to associate with Robyn was strewn about the room—

clothes, books, record dust jackets, a dozen stuffed animals.

"It's gone now, but when I got home after going to Laguna, it was sitting across the street, about halfway down the block."

"What?" I demanded. "I don't have the slightest idea of what you're talking about."

She went over to the window and peeked out. I saw that Robyn was serious, though I still wasn't following the conversation. As she turned around, I noticed perspiration, like glittering jewels, strung across her forehead. She spoke excitedly. "The detective's car. A blue one, like on TV. I don't know why they're always blue, but he was sitting in it reading a newspaper. I swear. He just left a little while ago."

"Why would he watch your house?"

"Because I think my parents are going to get a divorce. You know my dad. He'll build a whole file against my mother so he won't lose the house or me or anything. That's just like him. He always has to come out on top."

I gazed at her, puzzled. She kicked off her jeans and began wriggling into her swimsuit. It looked too small, but after she had it successfully in place, she paused, a defeated look on her face.

"I have to talk to you about this, Weeble. You don't mind, do you?"

I was exasperated. "Just tell me what is going on."

"Okay, from the beginning. Yesterday I was checking through my dad's desk for loose change. He always leaves a few spare quarters lying around. His checkbook was under a couple of letters, so I looked through that.

He has a way of cramming bills in the pocket. So what do I find, but a slip of paper with the name *Aimee* and a phone number." She stopped, as if everything were now explained.

"I'm really confused, Robyn. Can you make everything real simple for me? My head feels like concrete."

She went on unemotionally. "So I called the number, and a French woman answers. I know who she is, she works in his office. I've met her before. She's gorgeous."

"And you think your father is seeing this woman, huh?"

"I know he is because—" But the telephone ringing cut her off. She scampered out into the hallway and answered the extension. I tried to listen to her muffled talk, but my thoughts were skyrocketing. Little explosions burst about my head, sending jolts of pain down through my eyes. I felt a colossal headache coming on. Here I had come to Robyn for comfort and guidance, and now she was pulling me into a Sherlock Holmes script. Everything, I realized as I sat in the dark house waiting for her to return, seemed too unreal.

"Hey, it was Sissy," she explained when she came back. "She was going to call you later, but I said you were staying with me tonight."

"Robyn," I said, my face taut, "just tell me in plain American English what is going on, okay? A simple request."

"Sure." She acted hurt. "She was just going to invite you to a party at her house Friday night. I accepted for both of us. That's all right, isn't it? I mean I'll call her back. . . ."

"No, no, that's fine. I'm not busy Friday." I yanked her down next to me. "I just want to know about this mysterious stuff—you know, the detective, the French lady's telephone, remember?"

"You don't have to be sarcastic," she said.

"I'm sorry. I'm sorry, it's been a strange day. I guess I'm not following you very well."

We sat in silence, our emotions racing past each other, in different directions I was sure. I let her continue.

"Weeble, if you don't want to hear this, then tell me, okay?"

"I do. I'm sorry, go on."

"Well . . . paper-clipped to her phone number was a check for three hundred dollars made out to Hawaiian Village."

"What's Hawaiian Village?"

"I looked it up in the phone book. It's a beach complex in Laguna Beach. So I rode down there out of curiosity, and for the exercise," she added, "to see what the connection is."

"And?"

"And," she had a pleased, Columbo grin on her face, "I found out that unit one-oh-two-C is rented to a Miss Aimee Chanteuse. And while I was strolling around the complex, I saw my father and this woman—she can't be over twenty-five—lying on deck chairs by the pool, real cuddly, you know." Bitterness had slipped into her features. I thought she might start crying again, but she went on. "So it seems pretty obvious that he's got his girlfriend and he's paying for her apartment, and then he has the nerve to spy on me and my mother, and, you know, Weeble, I don't know who I hate the most. She's a drunk and he's a . . . liar," she spat. Then the tears came.

They were different from the last time, though. Instead of the uncontrollable agony of the child, Robyn's crying reminded me of someone who was so mad she didn't know what to do. She stopped and puffed three or four times like a runner who had just finished a race, and then she stood up. "Let's go swim. I have to get this out of my system."

"I'll listen more if you want me to."

"No, I'm all right. There's nothing more to talk about."

I quietly put on my suit. We went downstairs and through the dark house to the pool. She switched on a cheese-yellow light that illuminated the pool. The water was unruffled. I watched her dive in the shallow part and swim underwater to the eight-foot end. She came up coughing.

"Come on in," she called. "I've warmed it to bathtub temperature."

It was warm, almost too warm for swimming. I floated lazily on my back and watched the stars. The Big Dipper was brilliant. Orion hung over the roof like a bracelet.

"How far is a mile?" I asked.

"About sixty laps," she replied.

"You want to go first?" She nodded and then pushed off from the side, stroking with precision—a steady stroke, stroke, breathe; stroke, stroke, breathe.

I treaded water and began to count. She never eased off. Stroke, stroke, breathe—as regular and rhythmic as a machine. By the time she hit the halfway point, I was hanging on the side, doubtful if I could match her determination.

She began to slow down. Her hands didn't pull forward with quite the vigor, her kick became shorter, less frequent. I tried to study her face, but it appeared frozen, like stone. She plodded on emotionlessly.

I knew the pain inside was driving her. I marveled at her stubborn persistence. She wasn't going to quit with twenty laps left. And then she was down to ten. I could tell her legs were stiffening as she struggled through the final couple laps. Her knees were hardly bent, and her feet seemed to thrash awkwardly rather than propel her forward.

She coasted down the last thirty-yard length of the pool. Her hands shook as she grasped the side. It was a minute before she looked up at me. "I've always been afraid to go that far before," she said. "But I did it." She panted as she crawled up onto the deck and gagged.

"I doubt if I'll get half that far," I said.

"Go on," she wheezed. "Try it."

I was shaking before I began, just thinking about Robyn's exertion. After three laps, I had myself convinced a mile was impossible. Still I was curious how far I could go before I sank to the bottom waterlogged.

I stopped counting after ten. It was easier just to forget the distance and pace myself by breathing. As I stroked, I listened to my lungs, the steady rise and fall of the ribcage, which sent life-giving oxygen along my arms and legs. My heart thumped on like a faithful companion. After a while the water seemed to become more solid, or maybe my body was just settling into a new element. I thought it would hold me up even if I stopped stroking. Jell-O, I thought. I'm swimming in a pool of Jell-O. Strawberry, I hoped.

Along with the monotonous pull, kick, breathe, I thought of Nicky. There was a natural attraction between us, it seemed, although I had never admitted it to myself until now. I recognized that in the Mexican restaurant, how easy it was to be his date, his special lady. He was handsome and sensitive and affectionate, but we were like strangers in some ways. Some fragile balance had shifted between us, though, and I wanted the old Nicky again; but the new Nicky was so exhilarating and made me feel so alive. I didn't think Mom would understand. She would have been shocked to have found us on the floor. I hadn't expected anything like this to happen at all, but it seemed natural enough.

I caught Robyn's face on a turn. She was peering at me from far away, wrapped in a towel, wrapped in her own problems. How could I impose my confusion on her? It was an unthinkable idea. My mom loved me. Nicky loved me. I was the only one holding the many pieces of Robyn from flying apart. She needed my strength and love.

I tried to fight down the fear I had felt with Nicky. He had stirred a formless terror in me. I couldn't deny how special, how warm and excited I had felt when he kissed me, but maybe it was wrong. Maybe . . . I let the thought go. Weird images streamed in my head. I had never seen such intensely vivid colors, rising and falling like music, a symphony of starbursts, a kaleidoscope. My lungs beat like bellows. How far? How far, I wondered?

I pulled up in the middle of the pool. My eyes took a long time to focus. Robyn, wrapped in her towel, dangled her feet over the side. "How many?" I puffed.

"Seven more and you'll hit a hundred."

"Laps?" I asked, startled. The number took a moment to register. "That's over a mile. Why didn't you stop me?"

She shrugged. "I thought maybe you were going for a world record."

I glided to the side. My arms and legs were numb. My body felt weightless. I straddled the side with a leg and finally rolled myself onto the deck. The taste of chlorine was nauseating. I wanted to rinse out my mouth.

"Got anything to drink?" I croaked.

She helped me to my feet and we stumbled in through the elegant living room. The fizz of the cola felt like lava in my throat. I had never been so thoroughly fatigued. Every muscle of my body seemed to have collapsed.

I didn't remember climbing the steps to her bedroom. I was just suddenly on her bed watching the ceiling patterns merge into shadow. I said something that was insanely funny, which got us both laughing like psychos. The next morning, neither of us could recall what it had been.

Twelve

On Thursday evening, with Nicky still out looking for a studio musician's job, and Mom just finishing the rewarmed spaghetti I had made three nights before, I settled into a chair across the table from her and related what was happening in Robyn's family.

"Is she close to either of her parents?" she asked.

I nibbled at a hardened crust of garlic bread. "No, not really. Not to talk to, anyway."

"Who would she live with then if her parents split?"

"Her mom, I guess, though she says her dad lets her get away with more."

"That's really too bad," she said between bites. "It will be hard for her since she is so sensitive. I wish we could help, but it sounds like a sticky situation."

I stared at the nearly empty wine bottle in front of me. The label said 12 percent alcohol by volume. I wondered what that meant. My mom tried to glance at the newspaper as I continued.

"She says that we've already been a lot of help just for caring and listening and letting her sleep over when her parents are going at it. They've got such a beautiful house with so much furniture—so many things—but neither of them is happy. Robyn says her brother in college could care less what happens. I don't want to get that way—ever."

She looked up at me. "What dear?"

"I don't ever want to get that way," I repeated.

She patted my hand. "You won't. You're sensible. And I hope you won't rush off with the first guy who asks you, like I did. Take your time."

"You mean my dad?"

She gave a quizzical look, as if she were searching through her files. "No, you remember—Allen—the pilot who promised to fly me all over the world with him. I've told you that before."

"About when Grandma and Grandpa forced you to annul it?"

"Uh-huh. Don't you do that."

It had been a long time since we had talked about the past in Indiana. She didn't mind discussing what her life had been like, but usually she was so reluctant to elaborate that I never pushed my questions.

"When did you meet Dad then?"

"Oh Weeble, I've told you that a hundred times. Why don't I just make a tape recording, and you can replay it whenever you want."

"No, be serious, Mom. You always skip over that part."

She pushed away her plate and sat back with the wine

glass. "You'll make me remember how long ago that was. God, I was just a kid, seventeen when I got married. I met your father a couple months after Allen left for Chicago."

"Where was I?" I broke in.

"In heaven with the angels, you knucklehead."

"And how did you meet him?"

She shook her head at me. "I'm sure you must know this by heart now; I've told you enough times."

"But I like the way you tell it."

"Very well," she sighed. "I was working at this pizza joint—Romero's—when he came in. We got to talking and he asked if he could hang around until I finished my shift so we could walk home together. That's it."

"You skipped about spilling the pitcher."

"All right. I spilled a pitcher of soda on his shirt accidentally, well . . . almost accidentally."

"What do you mean?"

"Your father," she added, "was a great-looking guy. Tall, broad shoulders, dark hair, bronzed complexion—I wanted to be sure I made an impression." She smiled to herself. The best part of her memories went on inside her, so I could only imagine what she was thinking. "I moved in with him the next week, over my parents' objections. I was sure Dad would bring me back with a twelve-gauge, but they just stopped talking to me. It took them a couple years to forgive and forget. But you rescued the day: they both wanted a grandchild."

"I know." I smiled. "And I'm sure they wouldn't even recognize me."

Mom got up and began to clean the kitchen. I enjoyed

her reminiscing, but she never told me enough. The essentials about my father were something she never talked about. I really wanted to know what he thought about her, about me, if he ever wondered where his daughter was, did I have his eyes or dark hair.

"You want an ice cream cone?"

"No. I've got to keep in shape for cheerleading." I weakened when I saw her spooning out the cherry ice cream, though. "Maybe just a small scoop." It was rare to see her tired, but the perkiness was gone. She sprawled across from me, her arms flung limply on the table. "Mom, I don't want to sound dumb, but sometimes I feel like Snow White, you know?"

"Snow White? Why?"

"Well, maybe not Snow White, but I feel kind of abandoned, like lost in the forest. Oh, it's not your fault, you're a great mother. But, you know, I have this feeling inside like someone is coming, like I'm waiting for this . . . I can't explain it."

"Does it have to do with your father?"

"Yeah, in a way, I guess. I wish I could just send him a letter to tell him how I am, how school is. If I only had a recent picture of him, then he wouldn't even have to write me if he didn't want to. It seems so crazy that he's my father and he's alive somewhere and we don't even know where." Mom was silent. I wasn't hungry for the cone. An emptiness like a wide-open space rose inside me. It was a lonely landscape, the way the hills went on to the distant sky, the vast distant sky. It frightened me. "I'm going to find him someday. I promise, Mom; I'm going to get to know him."

"I know you hurt, dear," she finally said. "What happened between him and me is over. We simply weren't right for each other."

"What about me?" My throat was constricted. "I need to know who my father is. That's all."

"Well"—she looked up at the clock—"nothing we can solve tonight." It was like her to drop the subject when it came too close to the past, the past that was best kept at a safe, manageable distance. "I know Nicky can't really take the place of a father, but I agree it is great to have a man in the house, isn't it?" I stared through her eyes. They were doe eyes, fragile, deep set, all of a sudden glistening with moisture.

Yes, Nicky, I thought to myself. How little I knew about Nicky, how little I had touched beyond the affectionate exterior. He and my mother were so much alike. I didn't want to think about Nicky now, not when I had tried so hard to avoid him the past two days. Especially now when his tender face was intruding on thoughts of my father. I wanted to preserve what little I knew of him and the scraps Mom dropped glibly as if everything were over, finally and irreparably.

The front door clattered open. Nicky wrestled his guitar case through and stood before us grinning.

"Congratulate me," he said. "I got a job at RCA Records."

"Seriously?" Mom asked. When he nodded excitedly, she jumped up and waltzed him around the room. "You'll be rubbing elbows with all the stars then, won't you?"

"I ran into Linda Ronstadt today," he said.

I wanted to be excited, too, but I just sat and let them

raise the hoopla. Mom almost tripped over her feet, as Nicky bear-hugged her off the floor and whooped some more.

When Nicky released her, Mom wanted to know, "When do you start?"

"Monday morning. We're going to lay some background tracks, and then do promo's in the afternoon. I've *got* to get into the union now. I can't believe it!" He whirled an imaginary partner around the room. When he stopped he focused on me. "And you, little lady, are going to come along soon and meet some of these superstars. What do you think about that?"

I tried to be as enthusiastic as I could. "Okay, I guess."

"Yahooo!" he hollered. It took him another minute to settle down. "I may have to stay with you for a couple more weeks," he told my mother, "but as soon as I can, I'm going to take you and my little sweetheart to the best restaurant in California."

"Sounds great," my mom said. "And you know you can stay as long as you want. But I've got a date with an educator tomorrow." She shot a look at me. "So I best get on to bed. You too, Weeble."

I puttered around the kitchen until she was done in the bathroom. Nicky stared out the window toward the ocean, but the sky was overcast with no moon. I'm sure he couldn't see past the parking lot.

After I had scrubbed my face and teeth, I dashed for my room. Nicky sat on my bedroom floor flipping through record albums. "You like the New Wave?" he asked.

"Not especially." I didn't elaborate, hoping he would get the hint that I was tired.

He stood up and took me by the shoulders. "Want me to tuck you in?"

"No thanks." I looked away. Waves of heat shot up through my chest. I thought of ducking, but I stood immobile.

"Okay, good night, Blue Fairy." He bent over and kissed me on the nose. Then he was gone. A nest of snakes stirred in my stomach. For the first time in my life, I locked my bedroom door before I crawled into bed. I didn't know how I could be so in love with and so afraid of the same person.

Thirteen

I counted on a dull party at Sissy's. But I was surprised when I arrived at the plush Spanish villa nestled behind a stucco wall. Kids from school that I didn't think would even show up at Sissy's funeral loitered around the courtyard. A high school rock band was setting up equipment next to the pool.

"Must be nothing else going on tonight," I told Robyn. "Can you believe everybody who's here? Probably half the ninth-grade class."

"Including the skids." She nodded toward Jennifer, who was encircled by her usual entourage. Casey Blondell of the golden curls, hazel eyes, turn-me-to-butter smile, and the president of our class, had his arm around her waist. "Gosh, look at Sissy." She was headed our way.

"Oh, you guys," she gushed. "I'm super glad you

came." Her hair was flipped back on one side with an orchid. A slinky, low-cut Hawaiian print swirled about her.

"You really do up a party, don't you?" I said.

"My parents' idea. I just wanted to have a couple kids over, but they think I need more friends. They're into socializing and think I should be, too."

I recognized her father at the helm of a food table. He was directing a young Mexican boy in a white waiter's coat to place a tray of sausages by a huge punch bowl. The punch seethed, probably from a hunk of dry ice. Chips, crackers and cheese, slices of ham—the tables were full of munchies.

"Where's the band from?" I asked. I didn't know any of the musicians.

"Newport High," Sissy said, "Wait until you hear them. They have amplifiers that are going to blow the neighborhood right off this hillside. And the drummer is so cute. Too bad he's shorter than me."

"Everybody's shorter than you," Robyn said.

Sissy's mouth drooped. "I know. Sooner or later I have to stop growing. That's why I'm barefoot tonight." I looked down at her pink toes. She was not only taller than everyone, but her feet seemed enormous. She pulled the hem of her dress over them.

"You really do look exotic tonight." Robyn grinned. "I wouldn't have the guts to wear a dress like that."

Sissy hitched up the front. "Do you think it's too low? I feel a little self-conscious."

Her mother came up, and Sissy introduced us for the umpteenth time. She was one of those parents who came on you like sticky marshmallow but couldn't remember you from the next person, no matter how often you told her your name.

"Oh yes," she said to Robyn. "I think your father handles our account. Isn't he a very athletic-looking man with frosty hair, stops by the tennis club every afternoon for a quick set?"

Robyn nodded. "That sounds like him." She seemed to wince when Sissy's mother said "tennis club." That was an off-limits place for her about which her father was secretive. She glared at Sissy with obvious pain in her eyes. Finally Sissy's mother saw a familiar face she could accost, so she moved off.

"My mother supervised the punch," she explained, "and I think she got a little wacky from it."

"What's in it?" I asked.

"Mostly tropical juices—you know, in keeping with the South Seas theme—and some floating papaya, pineapple slices."

"Nothing intoxicating?"

"Not that I know. I think some of the basketball players over by the pool there already tuned up before they came." The group to which she referred did seem more raucous than usual. Periodically they captured a willing girl and threatened to heave her into the shallow end. It was still early, though, and everyone hung together in small groups talking. The band kept fiddling with electric cords, unable to get their equipment functioning.

Robyn ruffled the waist of her sundress. "I'm down ten pounds now. Can't you tell by the way this just *hangs* on me?" But our attention was drawn to Jennifer, who was laughing as though a parakeet had flown up her skirt.

"She makes me sick," Sissy frowned. "You think people would see how three-faced she is, wouldn't you?"

"Why did you invite her?" Robyn asked.

"Aw, her parents and my parents . . ."

"Hey—" Something struck me as I watched everyone milling around. Sissy and Robyn waited for me to shut my mouth. "How about this," I said. "We know there's nothing in the punch, but Jennifer doesn't. Let's all get slowly drunk, you know, real giddy, and tell her that it's laced with alcohol or drugs, shaving lotion, I don't care, but let her think we're not so straight after all. I bet her chin will drop to her knees."

"Couldn't we just cut the acting and go for the real thing?"

"No," I said. "This way, we can regain our composure when we need it. I don't want to act like a fool, but I would like to get her going. Want to?"

"I'd love to," Sissy grinned.

So we wandered over to the food tables and picked up a glass of the bubbling concoction. Robyn slurped it like a derelict. "Give it time to take effect," I cautioned her.

From time to time, Jennifer would glance our way, but then she'd turn back to Casey to make sure we saw how lovey they were with each other. By the third glass, I had begun to wobble slightly. Robyn was getting even more boisterous.

We edged closer to Jennifer's group. "Punch is tasty!" I smacked my lips. "Good punch, better try some," I called to her.

"I poured a whole bottle of rum in myself," Sissy slurred. "A whole, big, big bottle."

Jennifer's curiosity was up. She broke away from her friends and headed our way. "What's wrong with the band?" she asked.

"Just wait," Sissy blubbered. "Better than the Stones."

"Have some punch." Robyn thrust a full glass at her.

Jennifer took and sipped it. "Mmmmmmm, good. What's in it?"

"Gin," Sissy said. "A fifth of gin."

"I thought you said rum?" Jennifer asked.

"That too!"

"Yeah," Robyn added. "It makes your head go *worrra worrra worrra*, just like a brain grinder."

"A what?"

"You know, scrambles your head." I smiled.

She watched us weave drunkenly. I thought Robyn was overdoing her performance a bit, but Jennifer downed a glass and scooped up another.

"You and Casey pretty tight?" Sissy asked.

"He's such a darling, isn't he?" She studied the party. At least a hundred kids clumped together around the iron patio furniture at poolside, next to towering palms and yellow decorative jasmine pots. They were waiting for the music to start. Those closest to us stared, especially when Robyn stumbled back over for more punch. The Mexican boy jabbered something at her in Spanish, but she flashed him a wet smile and shook her head.

We kept drinking and making small talk until I felt that my stomach was going to float away. Finally the band appeared ready to begin. When the first chords rattled the red slate shingles, everyone applauded.

"I hope we can dance to them," Jennifer said.

"That's the idea," Sissy giggled. Her father strode by, but she turned away preoccupied. I watched Jennifer's face. She was still a little puzzled by our behavior, but I could tell she was waiting to see if the punch had any effect on herself.

The band was good. They started off with fast licks that nobody knew, then eased into a percussive medley that sent a few people bobbing in rhythm. The wait was to see who would be courageous enough to start dancing.

"Whoosh," Jennifer said. "The punch is starting to give me rushes." I caught Robyn's eye. We were both enjoying our charade. For once Jennifer was our prey. Casey came over and slipped his arm around her. She held the glass up for him to drink. He dribbled it down his chin like a baby. Jennifer began bumping her hip against his in time to the music.

"Wow, do I feel weird," Robyn sputtered. I was afraid that she might do something theatrical like pitch headfirst into the pool, but she turned to Jennifer and asked how she was doing. Jennifer kept up the hip banging and ignored Robyn. Robyn tried again. "You want to dance, Casey?"

Casey looked at Robyn as if he didn't comprehend what she had said. She repeated her question. This time he turned to Jennifer helplessly, but she only shrugged. I think we all about fainted, Robyn especially, when he unhooked himself from Jennifer and led Robyn over toward the band.

A cleared area in front of the band had been set aside for dancing. When Casey and Robyn began to move in time with the music, a half dozen other couples started to dance, too, as if the cue had been given.

I could tell Jennifer was stunned at being usurped by a "peasant." She floundered for something to say. "Yeah ... I guess the band is pretty good." Through the whole song she kept her eyes on Casey and Robyn.

Robyn looked great, I suddenly realized. She *had* lost weight. She was tanned and healthy looking, her hair feathered back just right. Her dress didn't so much as hang on her as it clung to her, in the right spots, with the pudgy bulges now gone. When the song ended, Casey kept her for another dance. Jennifer's eyes narrowed. She turned to see if anyone else could rescue her, but no one seemed to pick up on her distress. Except Sissy and me. We kept up our spirited patter.

"You getting off?" I asked.

"Ripped, really ripped," she smiled.

"How about you, Jenny?" She hated to be called Jenny. I said her name slowly to see her squirm. "More punch, *Jenny*?"

She gulped down her cup and walked away. I wanted to hug Sissy with laughter, but we were both intent on Robyn and Casey. They had locked together for the first slow dance of the evening. My stomach, as punch-full as it was, flip-flopped. Robyn, our shy, bumbling friend, was slow dancing with one of the desired "gentry"—one of the neatest guys in the whole school. And worse, she seemed to be enjoying it. I thought sure she was going to snuggle her head onto his shoulder.

Jennifer had found two girls who were lapping up every word she dripped. I felt sorry for the misguided ones who felt the need to hang on her. I could forget the shoplifting. I could probably even put up with Jennifer's phoniness. I hoped I was sensitive enough to understand that Jennifer did have some good qualities even though she hid them away. But I got furious when I saw others try so hard to please her, to be clever and liked, even when they made fools of themselves.

"Geez, nine o'clock already," I said. "I wonder how my mom's date with Mr. Blair is going?"

Sissy gawked at me like I had just spoken Spanish. "Your mom had a date with Mr. Blair?"

"Yeah, she's not that old," I said defensively.

"No, I didn't mean that. I think it's great, you know, I really do. Your mother seems so youthful—just right for him. I bet they make a cute couple."

The music picked up again, but we could tell Robyn was lost to us for the night. Casey had staked his claim on her. We watched Jennifer scooping a cupful at the watering hole. She sucked at the ruby red punch. When she rejoined the other two girls, I overheard her tell them that the punch was like white lightning. She doubted she could make it home if she kept slamming it down as she was. We had succeeded, but I didn't rejoice in the deception like I thought I would.

My thoughts were on Robyn. I felt abandoned by her. Even Sissy seemed in shock, mildly depressed. As we looked around the party, everybody appeared to have found their niche, busy with conversation or dancing. Only Sissy and I stared morose and silent.

I watched for another ten minutes until the first set ended. Robyn and Casey didn't come over. They stood down by the band talking. I thought of barging up to them, but when Sissy excused herself to search for someone, I headed for the gate. No one noticed me leave.

Fourteen

Our apartment was dark when I got home. I didn't expect Mom back until midnight, and it was only eleven. Nicky had gone up to Huntington Beach to check out a band at the Golden Bear, a rock nightclub. He usually stayed out until the clubs closed, around two. I almost always enjoyed having the apartment to myself—I could play music as loud as I wanted, talk on the phone without feeling guilty—but tonight I felt as if I had entered a mausoleum.

I switched on the television. After ten minutes, I realized I wasn't concentrating. I went into my room and put on an old record. Elton John sang a sad, lost-love song, putting me in an even more down mood.

I couldn't blame Robyn. Given the chance, I would have stuck my suction cups all over Casey, too. Who wouldn't? I was just surprised that he was interested in her. Not that she didn't deserve someone. She wasn't ugly. All her jogging and fanatic diets and calisthenics had slimmed her. And with the turmoil over her parents, she did deserve *some* happiness.

I clicked Elton off. His voice slowed to a gurgle as the turntable stopped. Music didn't help. I was restless. My room seemed cramped, drab, full of little-girl things. A broken music box propped open on the dresser held a dozen pairs of earrings. I removed the gold doves from my ears and dropped the posts in with the rest. Next to the music box Fuzzy Bear grinned at me, that stupid smile was frozen on his face forever. I stuck a pin in him, but he kept on grinning—a real glutton for pain.

I tried to console myself by remembering all the times guys had wanted to talk to me, and Robyn had been the odd person out. Now I knew what it felt like to be the room decoration. Strange, how so often I wanted transparency, to be able to pass unnoticed, but when the neatest guy in school chose . . . No, I didn't want to think that way. Robyn was my friend. I would stand by her, even if I had to feel like a fool.

The phone rang. I scrambled into the living room, but it was only a call for my mother. The lady talked with such a nasal twang, I could barely understand half the message. I wrote down her number and hung up, a little annoyed at being bothered so late.

I dug a cola out of the fridge, but it had gone flat. Leftover chicken, potato salad, ice cream that had crystallized, cornflakes, a box of raisins—I couldn't decide on what to munch. I poured a glass of wine and went back to my room. Mom would frown on my drinking her wine, and I knew it would make me a little high, but I was by myself.

When I couldn't think of anything to do, I usually went to bed. I unfastened the spaghetti straps on my dress and slipped out of it. Finding no clean pajamas, I pulled on an oversized football jersey. Number 34, green and white—it fit like a parachute.

Before I hit the lights and jumped into bed, I clicked Elton back on. A mournful song again about traveling on a plane for Spain. Apartment 202, below me, was quiet—a rare occurrence for a Friday night. I think I would have even welcomed their familiar clunking about.

A moth battered the screen, then flew off. A caravan of thoughts wound through my head. I tried to slow the jumble, but I was too hyped to settle down. I concentrated on Mr. Blair—the shape of his face, the gentle voice, the way he tilted his head when he was waiting for an answer to a question. I hoped he and my mother were getting on OK.

It was too early to fantasize something serious developing between them, but I didn't want him to think her weird or her to think him dull, not when I had to live with her and see him every day in school. Especially because I was at least partially responsible for their date. But I knew she would like him. Everyone did. He had a way of adapting his tone of voice and his interest to whomever he was with. I had seen him going on with a group of ninth graders as if he were one of them, and then suddenly transform himself into all business when another teacher or the principal wanted to talk with him.

And he had a lot of facets. I had known him for a whole year before I found out that he was a Vietnam vet. He was shy when talking about himself. No one realized he was such a skilled photographer, until his name appeared in the paper for winning some kind of award. I just hoped Mom wasn't running off at the mouth as usual and would give him a chance to talk.

I tried to get comfortable, but my bed felt like a sandbox. I think I had worn the jersey to the beach recently. When the Elton John record ended, I reached over and put on Emmylou Harris. For some reason her voice made me think of cotton candy.

A goofy image passed through my thoughts, about going to a midway when I was little back in Indiana. I remembered a gigantic fat lady chewing away on cotton candy, like a cow munching grass, and then I didn't see her for a while until I glanced up at the Ferris wheel, and there she was going around and around and throwing up the whole time.

It was a strange thought. I tried to dismiss it. A car pulled into the parking lot below. I used to be good at telling who had arrived by the sound of the engine, the way the car door slammed, shoes clicking up the sidewalk, but so many neighbors had moved in and out lately that I didn't know half of them. All I could decide was that a man had arrived.

I was trying to puff up my pillow to be more comfortable, when I heard the front door open. I sat up expecting to hear Mom pad in with a report for me. But I realized it was Nicky. He went into the kitchen and turned the faucet on. I could hear him singing faintly to himself. He shuffled into the living room. I don't know why, but I caught my breath, suddenly terrified.

And then his head was peering into my bedroom. "Weeble? That you? I thought you went to a party?"

"Yeah, but I left early." My tongue felt thick.

"What's wrong, Cupcake? You sound kind of down."

I sat up to look at him, but the backlight framed his head so I could barely see his face. He came a step into the room.

"No, I'm fine. I just felt like leaving early, that's all."

"Did something happen tonight?"

"No, well . . . kind of." I explained about feeling unwanted because of Robyn's abrupt departure. He listened, nodding thoughtfully.

"Hey, that happens," he said. "I'm glad for Robyn, but I know how you feel."

"I'll survive," I said, sighing. I pulled my legs up to my chest and watched him.

"You sure that's all it is? I'm good at detecting things."

"I'll be fine, really." I sounded unconvincing. He came a step closer and another until he was sitting on the edge of my bed. "How was the club?" I asked, uncomfortable at his sudden approach.

"Pretty good. Not as classy as I had expected; there was a noisy beach crowd in and they got pretty rowdy." He took up a strand of my hair. "I think . . ." He stopped and examined my eyes closely. "I think your eyes say that you're either very tired or still a little down. Now which is it?"

I shook my head. He smiled a summer meadow smile. Even in the semidarkness of the room it shot through me. "You know, Cupcake"—I didn't like the word; it sounded like I was dessert—"I wanted to talk to you about the other day. I'm afraid you got the wrong impression."

I tried to control my breathing. Mrs. Williams said

that breath control can relax your whole body. Mine felt like an overwound spring.

"You see," he continued, with his hand on top of my knee, "I sort of forgot that you were my niece for a minute. Not that what I did was wrong—no, it felt natural enough. You *are* a cute, sensitive female, and I'm—I admit it—a normal, healthy male who feels very attracted to you."

His hand had a way of creeping up to my neck. He drew my face closer to his. The fear had been replaced by a buttery warmth. His voice stroked away my tension. "I like to be totally honest, you know. And you're mature enough to understand what I'm saying, right?"

"It was part my fault, too," I said.

"No, no, it's nobody's fault. That's what I'm trying to say. You attract me. You do. I can't help that. We shouldn't feel wrong about what we feel inside. It's worse to deny our feelings."

I nodded. I would have agreed then if he had told me the ocean had just turned to marmalade.

"And I can't help the fact that your mother just happens to be my older sister. You know what I'm saying?"

"I think so. I've got it all pretty well worked out. I guess I feel the same way about you."

He kissed me lightly on the forehead. "I thought so."

I frowned. "I'm still a little mixed up, though."

"About what?"

"Oh, not really you." I couldn't find the words. The thought struck me that because he was older, he could take over the situation. For so many years I had been trained to relinquish control to someone older, that I wasn't troubled by Nicky's affections. I just didn't want him to push me farther than I was comfortable.

"What then?"

"I don't know . . . just strange inside. I've been thinking a lot lately about my dad, and then you came and I want to know even more."

"I understand that." He pulled me to his chest and stroked my hair. "I so wish I could fill up that emptiness," he said. "I feel kind of frustrated because I don't know what to tell you. I'm lucky I've had such a stable life, such loving parents. And I wouldn't say anything bad about your mother—Kathy is a dear lady, and I love her—but she's not a father, you're right."

He held me in silence. I listened to his heart beat, the rhythm of his lungs against my ear. I had never been closer to a man. My mother, even if she had wanted to, could never have held me so completely. I wanted to fall asleep in his arms, warm and secure.

He tipped my chin up toward his face. "You're precious to me," he whispered. And then he kissed my lips. I didn't pull back. I didn't even resist when he swung his legs around and nestled next to me on the bed. I closed my eyes as his gentle kisses explored my cheek and forehead, the tip of my nose.

I tried to just feel the soft pressure of his lips on my skin. It seemed like every pore of my body was awake. Every thought vanished. My head, whirring crazily a moment ago, had given over to the sensations my body was experiencing.

There was no desire to think or do anything but lie there and feel loved. I surprised myself by moaning slightly with pleasure. It wasn't wrong, Nicky had convinced me. It was right and natural. I did love him. And, for the first time in my life, I knew that a man loved me. I thought briefly of pushing his hand away when it slid over my breast, but his caress was unhurried and loving. His kisses on my neck tickled. "Am I going too fast?"

"What?"

"Too fast? I don't want to rush you into this."

"Huh?" I pushed up to my elbows. "Into what?"

"Into *this*, love—we're making love."

The words startled me. My breath stuck in my throat. "I thought there was a difference between the two."

He stroked my face again, but my body had already stiffened. "If we're going too fast, then we can wait on this," he said. He stopped and waited for a reaction. His eyes were wide and questioning. "Whatever feels right for you."

A squeaky voice, a little-girl voice: "God, I think I'm really mixed up now."

"It's simple, isn't it?" he began. "I love you. You love me, right?" I nodded hesitantly. "And," he continued logically, "when two people love each other they *make* love together as an expression of that love."

"Well, I don't make love with my mother," I said.

"That's a little different." He lifted his weight off me. My head was abuzz again, only now I felt that the emptiness was rushing over me like a twenty-foot wave. Nicky put the pieces together so simply, like one and one equals two. But something didn't make such easy sense to me.

"Nicky, I don't want you to stop loving me, but all of a

sudden, making love seems like sex, like you and I doing something that scares the hell out of me."

Both of us jumped slightly when a car door slammed in the parking lot. Our magic bubble had been pierced. Nicky was just Nicky and now staring down at me like he was going to beat me up.

"Are you angry?" I asked.

"No." He smiled, but the radiance was gone. "No, when you're ready to respond, you will. You have to listen to your head *and* body. Sometimes they don't say the same thing."

He was right. My body was drifting out of the room, but now my head demanded attention. It said unmistakably that my mom wouldn't approve of the position I was in with Nicky pressed against me. I modestly pulled my jersey down over my knees. "Nicky?" The little girl, toppling-over Weeble, spoke again.

"What?"

"I do need you to love me, but . . . but . . ."

"Don't worry," he said. "I understand." He stood up and sighed. "Just don't feel bad. And don't blame yourself for anything. What happened between us came from the heart. It doesn't change how I feel about you." He went out. I heard the front door shut quietly. He liked to walk alone on the beach. I was certain he was headed there.

I took a deep breath. It might have been the first one in what seemed like hours. I tried to fit together what Nicky had said about my head and my body and my heart, but all the pieces spun off into space like meteors. Only moments ago I would have sworn my body was about to levitate, but now I wanted to throw up. The face of the fat lady on the Ferris wheel came back. My head whirled in the darkness. A semi, gears grinding, whined along the Coast Highway, about where Nicky should be.

The clock ticked and ticked: the white rabbit vanishing toward Wonderland flashed past. And then my mother as the loony queen was shouting "Off with her head! Off with her head!"

I started to retch, but when I sat up and bent over, the sickness went away.

When Nicky explained everything it made so much sense. How did I get it so twisted and complicated, I said to myself. Why did I feel so rotten?

I knew kids in school who claimed to have had sex. That was nothing new. I could even name the ones who weren't exaggerating. A couple of girls went pretty heavy with older guys, maybe even guys out of high school. Nicky's being older did bother me a bit. And his being related was more of a problem, but I had seen him so little in fifteen years, that the word *Uncle* was more an abstract idea than the real person who could send chills along my back. There was more, but it whirlpooled about me so fast I was dizzy. Sometime between the wave engulfing me again and again, and my mother's face shaking me awake, I slept.

Fifteen

"Robyn's on the phone," she said.

I sat up groggy, trying to piece together my disconnected thoughts. I remembered last night—the party, Nicky's unexpected appearance, the grotesque dreams. It would have been easier to slump back into unconsciousness than to face the day ahead of me, but a faint loyalty toward Robyn stirred within me. I tried not to show the pain in my voice when I answered the phone.

"What happened to you?" she asked. "You just left me alone like a fool."

"*Me*," I said defensively. "That is a laugh. You didn't even know I left, you were so busy with the 'golden boy.'"

"You are mad, aren't you?"

I didn't answer. She was trying to get me to admit that I was wrong in leaving her, and I wasn't going to do it. I had reason to leave; she should have realized that.

"Well look, I'm sorry, okay? I didn't know that Casey was going to ask me to dance. I'm more surprised than anybody."

"The way I remember it," I said, "is that *you* asked him. We were pretending that the punch was spiked, remember, only you made it convincing, so don't try to tell me what happened."

She was silent. I felt ridiculous knowing that the thoughts racing through her head were going through mine too. I didn't want to make her feel guilty for finally having someone interested in her, especially since she was my friend. But something irrational made me continue. "I'm not mad, just a little disappointed that you'd ignore me like you did."

"I didn't mean to. I came to find you after the second set, but you had disappeared. We only danced together for a little while and then he went back to Jennifer. Boy was she pouty. You'd think they were married or something."

"So?"

"So that's all, okay? With you gone there was nothing for me to do but leave, too. I was going to call you, but I was afraid you'd be too ticked." She paused, then added, "Still angry?"

"Naw, a little upset, but not because of you."

"That's good. I didn't want you to hold anything against me."

"I'm not." I stared down at my face in the mirror. The eye shadow I had on the night before made my eyes look like I had been in a street fight. Dark and puffy, they blinked numbly.

"How come you're not talking if you're okay then?"

I dabbed at my lids with a tissue. "I said, I'm a little upset. Aren't you listening?" I could tell my sarcasm had struck.

"What do I have to do to say I'm sorry, stick pins in my arm?"

Now I felt guilty. "No, it's not you. I've just got something to work through. I didn't mean to snap."

"What's wrong?"

The face in the mirror was a little-girl face: the makeup was play makeup, as if she had gotten into her mommy's drawers and was pretending . . . yes, pretending. . . .

"Nothing." I listened to Mom banging in the kitchen: the coffeepot, a skillet, the toaster delivering its cargo. I couldn't stand early-Saturday-morning breakfasts. Nicky would still be sleeping.

"I thought you just said you were upset?"

"Well, yeah, a little," I admitted.

"Nobody is going to be home today but me," she said. "Why don't you come over, and I'll give you a crack at breaking your distance swim record. Want to?"

The aroma of percolating coffee smelled like mud—acrid, pungent mud. "Give me an hour to get ready and I'll be over."

"Bring Nicky if you want," she was saying as I put down the receiver. Had she said it, or had I imagined it? No, she definitely had told me to bring Nicky. How could I tell her my problems, I wondered, if she continued to be so ga-ga over Nicky? If she only knew him like I did, I thought.

Mom had her face stuck in the morning paper. She glanced up at me and then went back to her reading. "Want some pancakes, Pumpkin?"

I sat across from her at the table. She was perusing the wedding announcements, the pictures of a dozen smiling couples under her gaze. She looked up again. "How about scrambled eggs?"

"Ugggh! Don't make me sick."

"Well, how about going out for breakfast? We haven't done that in ages. There's a good omelet shop up on Bristol."

"I'm not hungry, and I don't see how you can drink that muddy water this early."

"Early? It's almost nine. It wasn't long ago when you'd be up at six every Saturday morning to see cartoons."

I watched the steam from the coffee cup swirl up and vanish. Mom leaned forward on her elbows. "How was your party?"

It was uncomfortable to meet her eyes. I stared down at the newspaper. "Oh, you know, about the same as any party."

But she wasn't listening to me. Something in the paper had caught her attention. "God, I can't believe that she's married again. And what nerve to wear a white wedding dress—who's she kidding?"

"How was your evening with Mr. Blair?"

She sipped her coffee. I couldn't judge from the expression on her face if she was pleased or just mildly pleased. Whatever the verdict, she definitely wasn't going to do handsprings. "A very nice man." A dud, I translated. "He's quiet." Who isn't around Mom, I thought. "But he was good company. We had a pleasant evening." She had said enough. My attempt to match them had failed. "Actually," she went on, "we did enjoy each other. We talked about you the whole evening, though."

"Me? What's there to say about me?"

"Oh, you'd be surprised."

"Come on, don't be so mysterious. What did you really talk about?"

"Different things."

"Are you going out again?"

She blew on her coffee, then hung her lip over the rim and sipped again. I wanted to gag watching her.

"I don't know. I'm not sure he's my type."

I had heard that response often enough. I was becoming convinced that "he's not my type" meant, I doubt if he would put up with all my idiosyncrasies or let me dominate the conversation so much, but if he was wealthy and in danger of dying, then I would see him again if . . . No, it was an unfair judgment. I think Mom simply wanted to avoid any entanglements that could develop into something more permanent. I didn't cross-examine.

"I'm going over to Robyn's."

"But dear, this is Saturday. We promised Nicky we'd go down to Capistrano and see the mission."

"You promised, not me. And besides, I've seen that old tumbledown church a hundred times."

"Weeble," she said firmly, "do it for Nicky. He's counting on your going along."

"Forget it," I growled. "I'm already busy."

She began to get angry. "I really think you should come. We had planned on visiting the harbor at Dana Point on the way back for lunch. You like the seafood restaurant there, don't you?"

"I don't want to go," I said stubbornly. "You and Nicky go if you want, but don't include me." The words rattled out faster than I had intended. Mom's face became flushed. I didn't give her the opportunity to reply.

After hurriedly dressing, I stomped through the living room toward the front door. Mom made no response, still bent over her paper as I went out.

The morning was crystalline, with no one stirring. I headed down the hill toward Robyn's neighborhood. A lazy dog yawned as I jogged past. I went by two little girls loading a baby buggy with dolls. At the first intersection I came to, I stopped to catch my breath. Maybe my outburst had been uncalled for, I reflected. I was sorry that Mom bore the brunt of my frustrations.

I wanted to scream, Why did Nicky have to complicate my life? Why me? And why was I ready to do anything for him?

I could see Robyn lounging out by the pool, with the straps to the top of her suit unfastened. I circled around the house on the garage side. She didn't hear me come up.

"Robyn!" I shouted.

She waved me over to where she lay. I folded my legs under me and sat down next to her. "What a weird morning. I already chewed my mom's head off for no reason."

She squinted up at me. "How come? Did she assault Mr. Blair?"

"No. I wish she had. Maybe I wouldn't feel like such an idiot then."

"It didn't work out?"

I stretched my legs until I could just touch the water. It was mild, perfect for a swim. "No, you know my mom. I thing she even could find something unsuitable with Robert Redford."

"Too old," she said.

I splashed my foot. I had left my suit at home, but Robyn had a couple of others I could borrow. I didn't feel like swimming just yet. As I sat in the sun, Nicky's warmth swept over me again. I began to tingle thinking about his closeness.

"What's Nicky up to?" She punctured my reverie. I looked over at her. Face relaxed, tanned, hair damp—she suddenly made me feel inadequate. For so long she had come to me with doubts and fears and troubled questions; now I was the weak one, full of confusion. I didn't like the reversal of roles.

"I'm still waiting for an invitation to come hear him play. Maybe he could even give me a few guitar lessons."

"You don't play guitar," I said.

"I will if he'll give me lessons." Her smile was unaffected. She didn't know—really know—Nicky. If she had, perhaps she wouldn't be so adoring.

"Robyn . . ." I couldn't find the right words. I didn't want to be unfair to Nicky. Maybe I was exaggerating what had happened between us.

"You're jealous, huh?"

"Hardly," I said. "Robyn, this is difficult for me to talk about, and I don't want you to get the wrong idea."

Her face changed. The lines around her eyes arched up with curiosity. I tried to choose my way carefully.

"I love Nicky, you know that. He's my mom's brother, right? But . . . well, he's a little too affectionate."

"Huh?" I hadn't gotten through to her.

"I mean, he . . ." I had to be blunt. "When I got home from the party last night, I went to bed. I was starting to doze off, and he came in—into my bedroom." Her eyes widened. "We didn't do anything, I mean—"

"He tried to rape you?"

"Oh no, not like that."

She continued to stare at me, puzzled. "So what happened?"

"Well, he kissed me."

She leaned forward. "Really?"

"I think I kissed him back." I stopped myself. "God, how dumb. I did kiss him back, but only because, I don't know—he was right there next to me, so warm and close."

"Really?" A faint smile tugged at the corners of her mouth. I could see her envisioning the whole scene. I didn't want her imagination to spring ahead of me.

"But look, Robyn, he's my uncle."

"I kiss my relatives."

"Be serious," I said. "Not like how Nicky and I kissed. But that's all we did. I'm just worried that everything could get out of control."

"For real?"

"Robyn, you're jumping to conclusions. He tried to explain how he felt, and it made sense. Boy did it! But now I'm more mixed up."

"Did you tell your mother?"

"Of course not. That would be stupid. She'd accuse us of all kinds of things. I don't think I could ever face her again if she found out."

She stared at me thoughtfully, and the excitement faded from her eyes. The telephone rang in the living room. She jumped up and ran to answer it. I slid closer to the pool so I could dangle my legs in the water. I kicked at the air bubbles drifting up from the filter. Robyn was the only one I had ever seen use the pool. Her parents never swam in it.

"Some people have nerve," she said when she returned. "How dumb do I have to be to not recognize a French accent. She acted so innocent, like 'Is Mr. Johnson available?' She caught me by surprise or I would have told her off. Back to your problem though."

A handful of gulls flew overhead. They screamed angrily and dove off beyond the rooftops. I leaned back as the water lapped against my knees.

"What do you think?" I asked.

"Well, if I were in your place I wouldn't complain, because I'm not related to him, and it would be all right."

"But it's more than that," I broke in. "Even if he wasn't my uncle, or almost ten years older, I still wouldn't know what to do."

"How did it feel?"

"What?"

"When he kissed you," she said.

I thought hard about my answer. I couldn't lie to Robyn. "Great. Fantastic! Like electric current running up and down my body. But when I thought about it, it didn't seem right. My body says yes and my mind says no. They're hooked together, but they're not in agreement. And it's my mind that is all knotted up now. What should I do?"

"I don't have much experience," she said.

"I don't want him to hate me, but I can't let this get worse or have Mom find out. What can I do?"

"Geez, Weeble, you know I'd do anything for you—"

"Volunteer to take my place, right?" But I had misunderstood where she was leading.

"No, please, I'm trying to be helpful." She paused to form her words. "If I could help, I would. I really don't know what to tell you, but I think you need to talk to someone."

"Sure, I'll go write to Dear Abby."

"I'm serious now. We can't joke about this, Weeble. I should have told you a long time ago, but when my parents started really blowing up I began talking to Mr. Blair. Just telling him about my family helped, you know. And he was concerned, but I didn't ask him to do anything and he never offered. Still, he has a good head, and we both know he's sensitive and . . . well, why not just talk to him?"

"Mr. Blair? Are you kidding? I'd have to transfer schools."

"Why?"

"I couldn't see him in the halls or in class after telling him all these wild stories about me and my uncle. No way am I going to tell him."

"Come on, Weeble, be sensible. He knows you and your mom."

137

"It's easy to say, Robyn, but I can't. I really can't. My mom just went out with him last night. He hardly knows your parents, but with me it's a lot more complicated."

"Then what are you going to do?" As concerned as she was, I could tell her patience was fading. Maybe nobody could help, I thought.

"I'm sorry if I ruined your day," I said, full of self-pity that I didn't deserve. "But I've got to get away and think. I'll talk to you later."

She followed me down the sidewalk. "Weeble . . . I'll come with you. . . ."

I motioned her back. "No, I've got to solve this on my own."

"But that's not fair. Why should you always play counselor to me and now you won't even let me help?"

I turned away and ran down the walk, my eyes filling with tears. There was no time for her to follow. I hurried down the hill toward the beach. When I got to the bathing area I headed along the cliff bottom toward a nearly inaccessible cove I knew would be deserted. I had to wade around the cliff's outcropping where it jutted out over the ocean, but the water was refreshing. As I had hoped, no one was on the narrow strip of beach that lay hidden from the more popular beach area. I sat on a large rock and dangled my toes in a tide pool. A hermit crab prowled lazily about the bottom of the pool. He ignored my toes and we shared the clear, cool water in harmony. I wished my inner self were half as calm.

My options were limited. I could remain silent and pretend nothing had happened. That was the easiest solution. But it didn't explain how I felt, and it surely didn't guarantee that Nicky and I would go on normally. How could I live in the same house with him?

Robyn had her own problems to deal with; I couldn't talk to my mom; and there was no one else, really. No one. For the first time in my life I felt like I didn't want a father, didn't care if I ever dated anyone. I hated men—the way they manipulated my feelings.

I started to cry again, then screamed in anger at the waves. I slumped to the beach and pounded my hands into the sand. After a while, when I realized how futile my outburst had been, I calmed myself by deep breathing. It was a peaceful spring morning. Gulls lazed overhead, searching the shore.

And then Robyn's suggestion came back to me. Mr. Blair. It did make sense. There was a special communication between us. He did know my mother, but more importantly, he was a man I could trust—probably the only one. He was mature and caring. Maybe he would understand me and Nicky. And I knew he would promise not to say anything to anybody, especially my mother.

Maybe I was just too mixed up to really care what he thought, but I was going to trust my intuition.

Sixteen

Fortunately, Mr. Blair was hosing off his car in the drive when I walked up. Had he been inside, I would have turned chicken and fled. I approached him nervously. When he saw me, he dropped his chamois to turn off the hose.

"Don't tell me you've come to chew me out for getting your mother home late," he said, grinning.

"No, I trust her with you. She said you were a gentleman and that you both had a good time. I shouldn't tell you, but she hardly ever says that about anybody."

"No kidding? I enjoyed your mother, and I promise my feelings won't affect your grade any."

"Not even a little?"

He laughed and squeezed out a wet sponge to throw at me. I ducked as it sailed past. With his shorts on he seemed less imposing than when he was dressed for school. I watched as he toweled off the windows. Because his car was a tiny import, he could reach all the way across it with one swoop.

"She's a great lady," he said. "We kept talking about you, though."

"That's what she said, too. What about me?"

"I'll never tell." He couldn't hide the teasing in his voice. Maybe because going out with my mother had revealed a new side to him, or maybe because he seemed relaxed and even more informal than he usually was, I felt confident that I could pour out my questions.

"I was just over to Robyn Johnson's house," I said. He nodded, but kept on with his drying. "And she . . . well, she mentioned that you had helped her about her, you know . . . her family?"

He stopped and looked at me. "I hope I've helped."

"She says you really have."

"I'm glad."

I decided the best approach would be to plunge right in. My hesitation was gone. "And I was wondering if you could help me with a problem?"

His face became concerned. "Sure. Let's go sit on the porch steps." His wet feet left tracks up the sidewalk as he led me over to the shady porch. I felt bad that my mother had not reacted to him more favorably.

When I was seated, I stared out across the street to the ballfield, where a young couple tossed a Frisbee. A tag-along dog was trying to intercept their saucer.

"So, what's up?" he asked.

"Well, my mother probably told you that her brother came to stay with us."

"Nicky, I think. He's a musician?"

"Uh-huh, Nicky. He's the problem."

"You're not getting along?"

I wished the problem had been that simple. Nicky—the Nicky I had imagined in Indiana—had turned out to be much more than I had expected. I hoped I wouldn't sound foolish as I tried to explain.

"Well, yes and no."

"A multiple choice answer," he joked.

He made me feel like I could tell him anything. "Actually, we get along great. He's a very loving person, but—I hope this makes sense—he's a little too loving. I mean, he's started kissing me and things."

"And things?"

I related about being in bed after the party when Nicky came into my room. I expected his eyes to widen with interest, as Robyn's had, but he listened calmly, as if I had been telling him about an incident in the school cafeteria. When I finished, he spoke softly.

"The important thing to remember about your feelings is that they're always very complex. Like algebra, there's nothing very simple about them."

"Boy, that's for sure."

"But feelings are neither right nor wrong; they're just feelings." He stopped, aware that he had lost me. "You're confused."

"What can I do?"

He massaged his foot. Because he always wore pants in school, I had never seen his legs. I was surprised how tanned and muscular they were.

"I think your mother should know."

I shook my head. "I can't tell her that her own brother is some kind of pervert."

"You don't have to say that. He didn't actually rape you, even though it seemed apparent he was leading in that direction."

"That's just it," I said emphatically. "I'm afraid I encouraged it."

He shrugged. "The thing to do then is to get it out in the open. Regardless of what you feel, the situation won't go away. You have to deal with it now."

"I don't think my mom will handle it well."

"Weeble, if *you* love them, you've got to be honest about what's bothering you."

"If only Nicky hadn't come . . ." But it was a stupid thought, and I knew it as soon as the words were out. We didn't say anything for a long time.

Finally, he repeated gently, "*You* have to deal with this. Don't underestimate your mother, either. As I listened to her last night, I could tell she thinks a lot of you. You're her best friend. Whether you admit that or not, she depends on *you* for emotional support. Don't you think that support should be mutual?"

I could see his point. I wasn't giving my mother much credit for understanding. She might blow up at first—that was normal enough. But I knew she would be able to handle anything I told her, no matter how difficult for me.

"I'm not passing judgment on anyone," he continued. "But I don't think the physical affection that's developing between you is good for your mental health."

"I've been like a schizo lately," I admitted.

"Then confide in your mother. I bet she'll take it better than you think."

He was right. I only needed the courage to bring it up.

So long as I hadn't gone all the way with Nicky, I didn't need to feel guilty. Still, I didn't want to betray Nicky. I didn't want to lose his trust or his love, but Mr. Blair was right. If Nicky did love me, *really* love me, he wouldn't want me to be all twisted up inside. And most importantly, I didn't want to hide anything from my mother.

"I'll do it. She may kick me out of the house, but I'll tell her."

"She won't." He grinned.

He walked to the street with me and put his arm around my shoulder to give me a half hug. "Don't fret," he said. "Life doesn't get any easier."

"Thanks," I said sarcastically.

All the way back to Robyn's house I felt warm and sure of myself. Mr. Blair had demanded nothing of me, but he had given so much. I wondered how I could ever repay him.

Robyn listened raptly as I told her everything we had talked about. She agreed that Mr. Blair had offered sensible advice. "Isn't he a darling?" she said, as if drooling. "Too bad he's not ten years younger." That, I figured sadly, would make him almost Nicky's age.

Mom and Nicky weren't home by late afternoon. I wandered about the apartment aimlessly, a thousand doubts nagging my thoughts. I tried to resurrect the confidence that Mr. Blair had instilled in me, but the longer I was alone, the more I shriveled back into confusion. My mother's shocked voice whined in my head: How could you? How disgusting! Right under my own roof? Or worse yet: Weeble, dear, what a vivid imagination you have. How in the world can you insinuate such a thing about my baby brother? I was slowly losing ground. The cliff edge yawned in front of me. There was no way to go but into the dark, the jangled daze of silence and fear and lies.

"You should have come with us," were her first words when they returned. "You missed a great shrimp lunch, didn't she, Nicky?" She flitted in with a sack of groceries. Nicky trailed her, an amused expression on his face.

"Yeah, we missed your company today," he said.

I told them where I had been all day, but I was not in the mood for small talk. Nothing interested me in my room, so I went into the living room to see if Mom had picked up any new magazines.

Nicky got out his guitar and fiddled around tuning it. I got up to see if we had any frozen pizzas in the freezer. Mom was flipping through the mail.

"How come you're so mopey today?" she asked.

"I don't know. Just bored, I guess."

"Well, you could have come along."

The inside of the icebox looked like an arctic cavern. "How come the freezer is never defrosted?"

"Anytime you feel like doing it," she replied, "be my guest."

I peeled a hard-boiled egg and took it into my room. From a stack of teen magazines, I removed a well-worn issue. John Travolta, a sexy look in his eyes, stared through me from the cover. It was over a year old. I threw nothing away. Looking around the room, I felt like a miser.

I waited for an opportunity to talk privately with my

mother, but none developed. She was balancing her checkbook when I peeked out, and Nicky still kept plunking away on his guitar. He acted a little distant, almost disinterested in my popping into the living room. I stood with my hands on my hips for a minute, then went back into my room.

The words and pictures of the magazines blurred together. I snoozed off for a bit. When I awoke, a stale taste in my mouth and the room spinning down slowly made me a little sick.

Mom stood in the half-light of the door. She was dressed to go out.

"What?" I sat up, groggy.

"Nicky and I are going out for a while. I want to show him a couple of clubs in Newport Beach. You want us to bring you a pizza or anything?"

"Uh . . ." I tried to stitch up my unraveling thoughts. "I . . . uh . . ."

"We shouldn't be out late." She turned to leave.

"Mom?" I raised my arm. It felt like a dead tree limb. "I'm kind of sick."

"Really, what's the problem?"

"I don't know. My stomach's upset." I lay back waiting for the familiar hand on my forehead.

"Probably because you didn't eat anything all day. You kids! So worried about losing weight at your age."

I pulled my knees up to my chest.

"You want some Seven Up or anything?"

I didn't say yes or no and could see that she was deliberating whether to stay home after all.

"Well, hell," she sighed. "I'll tell Nicky to go alone so I

can stay with you. Why don't you put your pajamas on and climb under the covers." She went out to inform Nicky she was staying. I was waiting under the covers when she returned. She sat down at the foot of the bed. The sound from the front door closing vibrated the walls. Although I really did feel sick, I didn't like to manipulate my mother like that.

"You know, I think these cheerleading tryouts are bothering you," she finally said.

"No, not really."

"And then you've taken Robyn's problems on yourself."

She had it all figured out, only wrong. I pulled together my failing courage and blurted out what happened after the party. She listened quietly until I finished.

"Was that the only time?" she asked, her voice hard.

I told her about the time on the living-room floor.

She stood up and began to pace—predictable enough. "Oh God," she muttered to herself. I expected her to add Why me? but she didn't.

"You're making this up," she said.

I began to churn inside. She was betraying me, and the pain I felt started to flood my eyes. "I'm not, I'm not. I wish I was," I cried. My face twisted up tight like a little girl's.

"Then you're exaggerating. Nicky wouldn't try that—he's almost twice your age. He wouldn't take advantage like that."

I dragged my arm across my eyes, smearing tears all over my face. I couldn't answer. There was controlled anger in her voice. She surprised me: no hysterical outburst, no disbelief, just the cold certainty that my imagination was running wild.

"Let's just drop this little conversation, Weeble, and pretend it never happened, okay?"

But I detected the first faint doubt in her voice, almost like she could unmake the truth by saying it. There was a question still hanging in the air between us.

"Mom, I'm not exaggerating."

She looked at me, clear through me. A deep sigh, then she sat next to me on the bed.

"Let's start from the beginning again."

So, painfully, I once more choked out what I had told her. She stroked my hair as I spoke. She didn't interrupt. After I finished she sighed again.

"Maybe you've confused your need to be accepted by him with romantic love. I'm not saying you don't have real feelings, sexual feelings even, but Weeble, my God, do you know what you're accusing my brother of?"

I felt like all the breath had been squeezed from me. I couldn't avoid the truth anymore, nor could my mother. "It happened just the way I told you."

She frowned. Perhaps she wasn't quite convinced I was telling the whole story. "You're sure you didn't give him any reason to—"

"I don't know," I broke in.

She patted my knee. "At your age it's easy to confuse infatuation with real love."

"Mom!" I said sharply. "I've never lied to you before." Then, uncontrollably, the tears came again, shaking my whole body.

She smoothed the hair back from my forehead. It was

damp and my face was a mess. "I believe you, dear. He did say 'make love'?"

I nodded, sniffling, then wiped my nose on my sleeve. "It's all my fault." It wasn't though. I wanted it to be, but it wasn't.

"He's older. He should know better," she said protectively. "What the hell could he be thinking, anyway?"

The pain kept coming from so deep inside I didn't think it would ever end. I wanted her arms to wrap me consolingly, but she stood up and began to pace. I hugged my knees to my chest.

It was just as well Nicky wasn't home. Mom probably would have flown into him without sufficient time for reflection. Now, she had all evening to think things through.

After a minute of pacing, she flung her hands up into the air. "He'll have to leave. That's the only solution. I wish it wasn't true, because he's my brother, but he can't stay now."

Satisfied that she had the problem worked out, she went into the living room and switched on the television, but I doubted if she paid much attention. I tossed for another hour until the hurt subsided and my stomach began to feel better. Mom paid no attention when I went into the kitchen for a refill of Seven Up. I sat down next to her on the couch.

"Mad at me?"

She patted my leg. "No, no, it's not your fault. I am disappointed in Nicky, though. I really didn't know what to expect when he came out. I hadn't seen him in so long. God, it would kill Mom and Dad to find out about this."

I stared at a hokey shoot-out in an old Western. Cardboard Indians whooped past a wounded cavalry train. Periodically, a stuntman would tumble from his horse.

"I guess . . . I needed to feel close to a man," I said brokenly. "It felt—at first—so right with Nicky."

"We all need closeness and even intimacy," Mom said. "Especially with the opposite sex."

"But I've never known that," I said.

"I know. Sometimes I've wished so much that you had a father, that everything had worked out. And I'm not even saying that it's wrong for him to kiss or hold you, but . . . It's hard to explain."

"You don't need to," I said. "Now I realize that Nicky is as mixed up as me."

"That could be." She put her arm around me. Loving gestures from my mother were rare, so I snuggled against her. We watched the program in silence for a while.

Nicky returned about eleven—earlier than we had anticipated. Mom shooed me into my room, but I kept the door cracked. I could tell from the tone of his voice that he was bubbly. Mom circled him.

I expected more of an angry accusation, but she only said, "Do you know what you've done to Weeble?"

"What do you mean?"

"I mean kissing her in her bedroom—you want more?"

"What?" He was playing it cool, unruffled.

"Come on, Nicky, I'm your sister. She's your niece —a fourteen-year-old kid. Why do you want to get her screwed up about love? Why the sexual come-on with her?"

"Hey, I love her, all right? Any crime in that? She is my flesh and blood, just like you."

My hands were sweaty and white against the dark wood grain of the door. I edged it open a little farther so I could follow my mother's pacing.

"Are we talking about family love or male-female love?"

"Are you serious?" he replied. "She *is* my niece. You think I'm some kind of sicko or something?"

"I'm not saying that. I just don't like what is happening in Weeble's head now. She's a confused girl. Adolescence is difficult enough without this."

But I had heard enough. I had heard *the* lie—Nicky's lie. It split through me like a lightning bolt. He had implied that he was the innocent, wounded party. That was clear enough. After all, I was his niece, he had said. I thought back: all along, the feelings in me had been real. What had been inside Nicky, I didn't know. All I knew was that I hated him, and the words burst from me as I charged into the living room.

"You liar, you liar," I screamed. I would have hit him, but my mother blocked the way. They were both startled.

"Weeble, go to your room," she said firmly.

I saw Nicky's face through blurred eyes. "I thought you loved me," I blurted out.

He worked the words over in his mouth as silence crackled in the air about us. "You're a kid, Weeble. You really didn't think that I—"

"You lied to me, Nicky," I interrupted. His eyes had grown small and dark. I wasn't going to let him retreat into himself or manipulate my feelings any further. "And you're still lying, so don't say any more. She knows all about it."

151

"She's never lied to me before, Nicky. What you did to her was wrong, so don't make things worse."

He started to sputter something. He stopped and looked at both of us, his mouth hard. "It could have been good between us—all of us," he said, emphasizing the final *us* and looking coldly at me.

I was suddenly scared of him.

"God, I pity you," Mom said sadly.

He looked at her with hurt in his eyes. There was nothing more to say. He shook his head and went into his room. Within ten minutes he was packed and out the door without another word.

Mom went into her room with a drink and shut the door. I wanted to be close to her, to lay my head against her lap, but she needed to be alone.

I tried to settle back into bed. If I ever saw Nicky again, things would never be the same between us. That hurt. But I was relieved in a way.

Mom would probably play down the whole drama, I thought, and within a couple of days ignore that it had ever happened. She was like that. The confrontation had cleared the air, but we had all lost something valuable.

I listened to the noises outside my window gradually tick down toward morning. In the distance, a dog howled forlornly. His cry echoed inside me.

The next morning my mother treated me like an invalid. She brought me breakfast in bed, fluffed my pillows, and volunteered to fill a bath for me.

"I'm not sick, Mom," I said.

"I know. Just trying to do something nice for you."

It was her way of trying to make up to me for some reason, and I didn't like it. I kicked back the covers and sat on the side of the bed.

"Well, how about if we go shopping, then? We haven't done that together in a long time."

And we hadn't, either. I didn't want to feel guilty by refusing her, so I agreed. She was trying too hard, I told myself as I got dressed.

Neither of us said anything about Nicky or the evening before as we drove toward Newport Plaza. We had survived the night, that was enough.

The mall was just beginning to open, and only a few Sunday shoppers had arrived. A tropical breeze rustled the palm fronds of the trees in the center walkway. Sunlight sifted through the branches, and birds from the pet shop chorused noisily. I was still numb inside, as though my whole body had been immersed in Novocain. I floated along at my mother's elbow, only half aware of what she was saying.

She led me into a clothing store. Racks of summer dresses, so colorful and attractive on mannequins, seemed to hang on me like hand-me-downs.

"Don't slouch, hon," my mother was saying.

"I think it's so cute on her," the saleslady was adding.

"Try this one," someone was saying, as a new dress was thrust into my arms. I felt suddenly faint in the small changing room, like the walls were tumbling in on me. My heart pounded in my ears; the air was too thick to breathe, suffocating.

I rushed out of the shop and into the cool of the morning. Bird song. The wind off the ocean carrying salt scent. Feet clicking past. My mother's hand soft and comforting on my neck as I bent over my knees and tried to focus on the ground.

"Are you all right? You look a little flushed."

My sandaled feet swam into view. My toes, so far away, seemed unfamiliar—as if attached to someone else's feet.

My mother's hand was steady on my neck, stroking along the nape and onto my bare shoulders. I inhaled and tried to sit up. People eddied past, but we were invisible to them.

"Feeling any better?" My mother said, her voice steady like her hand.

Gradually the ground slowed, as my thoughts merged into something recognizable. I was brought back by my mother's hand, on my neck, directing my head to its point of balance, soothing the confusion away.

"A little dizzy," a faraway voice said. As I breathed deeply, I realized it was mine.

"Just catch your breath," she said. "Get your bearings."

My skin tingled all over. Perspiration had broken out on my forehead. I let the breeze dry it.

"That's a cute swimsuit in the window," my mother said to no one in particular. I looked at the shop windows, but couldn't find the one she was referring to.

After another minute I said I was sorry for rushing out. I was always apologizing, it seemed, as if I were responsible for the whole world. It's the social worker in me, Robyn would say.

"You couldn't help it, dear. Just take your time, and when you feel better, let me buy you a dress."

"I don't want a dress," I said, unsure where the quick response had come from.

"Then you can pick out a new blouse."

"I don't want anything."

I listened, but the only sound she made was her lungs, rising and falling softly. Had I hurt her feelings?

She put her arm around my shoulder, and I almost shook it off, but I let it rest there. People went past, but we stayed invisible, wrapped in shade on the bench. I knew what she was going to say before the words left her mouth.

"We've been through a lot together, Weeble. We've weathered a lot."

"I know."

A eucalyptus leaf fluttered to the ground, too green and too young to have fallen so early in the summer.

Her arm tightened about my shoulder. "We both hurt now." Her lower lip trembled slightly. "I'd do anything for you."

"I know."

I saw her eyes moist over and then there was no need for words. She hugged me to her spontaneously as our tears came, and she held me, still invisible to everything about us, as the healing flowed from her to me and back to her like a million volts of love.

Seventeen

On Friday afternoon, after a rigorous week of workouts, Robyn and I prepared for the cheerleading finals. We met by my locker after the last class. I dumped all my books and notebooks in under a shower of fresh gym clothes. Today was not the day to be rumpled, because, even though we were tense, to show our nervousness was as much to doom ourselves to failing. Our appearances had to shine with confidence. We had to go through the tryouts as if we already had been chosen. Every flaw would be spotlighted before the crowd of two hundred students, loyal parents, and teachers. And right at the foot of the bleachers, the judges would scrutinize each girl for her buoyancy and poise, her execution, vocal qualities, and that nameless ingredient that separated the top six from the competent twenty-four girls who had lasted the preliminaries. I reminded myself that I had survived the grim competition last year.

Robyn was in the depths of negative thinking as she waited for me. "I'll never make it to the gym," she moaned. "My legs are too wobbly."

"I'm scared, too," I said. "But fear is supposed to make you perform better."

"I should be fantastic then!" Only her mouth puckered, as if she were trying to turn her face inside out.

"Relax," I said. Some of the eager contestants were already dressed. They ran by us in the hall toward the main entrance, where groups of students jostled each other before the gym was opened to spectators. We hurried silently to the locker room.

Robyn pinched my arm as we entered the bedlam of girls preparing to do battle. "Look over there." She pointed to three girls in the corner near the shower stalls who were energetically pacing themselves through a routine. Jennifer, her face taut with concentration, pumped her arms in rhythm.

"She's a shoo-in," Robyn said.

"Nobody is. We all have to do the same three cheers. If you mess up any one, no matter who you are, you might as well forget cheerleading."

"Well, I'd settle for alternate," she said, attempting to smile. The smile took too much effort, though. She dropped to the wooden benches and held her head. "I can do it great at home, alone. But I know I'll blow it with everyone watching."

"Just imagine there's a mirror between you and the audience. All you'll see is yourself. Just block them out."

Mrs. Williams, clipboard in hand, announced that all contestants should be warmed up and ready to begin in ten minutes. I fought with a knot in my tennis shoe. Robyn began to wriggle out of her jeans, her eyes shifting about the room. I couldn't help but stare at one girl who wore a T-shirt that probably belonged to her eight-year-old sister. I was sure the seams would split with the slightest tension. Other girls wore shorts that added a new meaning to *short*. The male judges were not immune to these extra flourishes that some of the girls resorted to.

"What if I throw up in front of everyone?"

"You won't." I was becoming impatient with her. By the time I got my shoes laced up, she was strutting in front of the mirror with her shoulders thrust back awkwardly. "You look like a rooster."

"Good posture's important," she explained. "It helps your breathing."

I pulled my hair back and tied it. Side by side in the mirror, we looked like sisters. The sun had bleached out her normally dark brown hair until it was almost the same honey gold as mine. With ten pounds shed, she appeared taller, more athletic. What I had fortunately been born with, she had worked hard to achieve.

Noticing the comparison, she smiled. "The old body is in pretty good shape." But her expression changed abruptly. "Inside I still feel like a clumsy slob."

I held out my hand for her to shake. "We're both going to make it, right?"

She took my hand gingerly. "Do we still have to go off the end of the Newport pier if we don't?"

But we were interrupted by Mrs. Williams's final call. The group filed out of the locker room to head for the gym. I stopped at a drinking fountain on the way to wash out my cotton mouth. When I stood up, Mr. Blair was right behind me.

"You know, there's talk among the teachers that we should have two squads of cheerleaders—one for the winter and one for the spring sports," he said.

"I'm going to make this one," I said determinedly.

"That's the attitude!"

I edged by as he bent over for a drink. "By the way, how's the home front?"

"Better. Nicky's got his own place in West L.A. now. He moved a couple days ago."

"And your mother?"

"Okay. She hasn't said much lately—still upset, I think."

He nodded as I was pushed into a stream of bodies. Robyn stood outside the gym door, paralyzed when I reached her. One whole side of the gym was filled with spectators, nearly twice as many as I remembered from last year. Groups were shouting out the names of their favorite girls. Huddled around Mrs. Williams, those who were trying out seemed intimidated by the boisterous crowd.

"We want it quiet!" Mrs. Williams called for attention. "We don't want you shouting out names, even though we appreciate your response. The girls are nervous enough without having to yell over you," she told the audience. A couple of mothers in the front row tittered. "And thank you for coming, parents."

The eight judges took their places at a long table set up in front of the bleachers. Four of the judges were male teachers, four female. Mrs. Williams abstained from voting unless there was a tie that needed to be decided. The judges were supposed to be impartial, but that was an impossible task. They, like the crowd, had their favorites.

To highlight the contestants, the girls would come forward in groups of three, prance about, do three mandatory cheers in unison, and receive applause, until all twenty-four had the opportunity to show their skills.

I was not surprised when my name was called for the first group. Robyn slapped me on the back as I struggled forward. I felt like I was moving underwater, every motion painful and deliberate. I had to be more spontaneous. I needed zing. Do it now or never, I said to myself. The first cheer—the easiest of the three—was routine for me. I had done it a thousand times in my sleep. We began to count. I mirrored the movements of the girls on my right and left perfectly. My cheer was firm, but there was nothing spectacular about it.

We lined up for the second routine. Just as we began the count, I happened to notice someone shove through the group clustered at the door. It was my mother. I lost count of my steps. When we went up for the leap I muffed the yell, my voice cracking in the middle. I landed on the polished wooden floor a split second behind the other girls. The crowd knew what I tried to fight out of my thoughts: I had blown my chance.

I glanced over at my mother, but she stared impassively. The judges hunched over their tabulation cards making notes. I tried to psych up for the final cheer. Was it worth the effort? I couldn't let anyone see my disappointment, especially the judges. I mustered up a phony smile, one that Jennifer would have been proud of.

As we took our positions for the third routine, I visualized how every part of my body would move. I could see only myself in the mirror, the huge mirror that stretched invisibly between myself and the anxious spectators. Not even my mother was visible in the reflection. One, two, three—we began. I summoned every fiber of energy, and when the leap came, I felt like a gazelle springing over the heads of everyone, rising toward the ceiling. My own shattering yell brought me back to the floor, in front of the judges, where I was poised in a perfectly executed split. I returned to the waiting group, still dazed.

"You did it!" Robyn thundered in my ear.

I shook my head. Even a minor slip would be recognized and noted. Among twenty-four hopefuls, an opportunity had to be seized. There were no second chances. My turn was over. I didn't feel the jubilation like I had the previous year. I knew I had failed as certainly as I knew I had won a year ago.

The next group went on to perform. I tried to avoid looking at my mother, but I couldn't. She had not told me she was going to take off work early to come. That was unlike her. If I had known, I wouldn't have been surprised, I wouldn't have lost concentration. But I refused to blame her for my failing.

The routine of the second three girls was flawless. The next three paraded out. Wild hoots greeted them. The girl with the tight T-shirt didn't mince around. She stuck her chest proudly into the air. The girl on her left was so nervous, she could only yelp instead of shout the words. The judges wrote furiously between routines. They were businesslike.

Robyn pulled my arm after each group finished and said that this girl or that one had it made. By her count, nearly half of those nominated would be chosen.

My mother's unexpected presence kept coming back to my thoughts. It was so unusual for her to let anything come before her job, but I knew why she had come.

My hopes of still being chosen dwindled as I followed the adept movements of each candidate. Even some of the least-popular girls performed with fervor and stumbled back to the waiting group exhausted.

The crowd was gracious with mistakes and loud with pleasure when the most attractive girls finished in splits before the judges' table.

Robyn's name was called with the second-to-last group. Jennifer was also one of the three. I tried to catch my mother's eye, but she was watching intently. There was no hesitation in Robyn. She strode out to the middle of the gym ready to begin. Jennifer stood next to her and waved at someone in the bleachers.

I tried to study their movements as the judges did. Were they polished? Did they communicate to the fans? Were their movements bouncy and zesty? How did their voices carry?

Robyn emitted a deep, resonant yell that startled even her. If Jennifer was the popular favorite, Robyn was at least the most outstanding and vigorous in her attempts after the first two cheers. Jennifer messed up the final routine by jumping out of step then tangling her feet. I was curious how the judges would mark her. The spectators' response was deafening, but I couldn't tell if it was for Jennifer or Robyn, who had been terrific.

Sissy was in the last group. She was precise and energetic, but just too tall to ever be chosen. Maybe if she stopped growing, the other girls would catch up to her by tenth or eleventh grade.

Mrs. Williams announced a ten-minute break to tally the results. I cringed when I saw my mother headed in my direction. She was exuberant. "You *were* great!"

"I don't think so. It should have been better."

"Well, I'm satisfied," Robyn interrupted.

"You should be," my mother said. "You acted like a different person out there, less timid."

"I can't believe it," she said. "Even though I won't make the top six, I feel really good that I stuck with the tryouts, and I did the best I could."

I went over to the bottom bleacher and sat down. Robyn, then my mother, followed me over. I expected Mom to be consoling, but she didn't mention the slipup. She was watching the judges' table when I looked up. Even Mr. Blair, I realized, couldn't overrule the other seven judges.

Everyone milled about in anticipation. I thought of excusing myself to go to the locker room, but I knew I had to stay and congratulate the winners. Mom sat down next to me. "Whatever the decision," she said solemnly, "I'm glad to be your mother." I thought her eyes were misting up. I looked away. It was the first time she had ever taken a real interest in something I was concerned about. I squeezed her hand.

Mrs. Williams waved people back to their seats.

"Everyone was superb," she said. "But we can't choose you all. The judges have decided on the following for next year's tenth-grade cheerleading squad."

The first name she read was Sissy's. I was astounded. She had been good, exceptional even. I was glad the judges didn't penalize her height. The next three girls were obvious choices. Each was cute, talented, and popular. Waiting for the fourth name to be announced, I knew I had failed. Next year, I said to myself.

Mrs. Williams read, "Robyn John—" and then a shrill explosion went off in my left ear. Robyn had been chosen. She sprang into the air still screaming, and then she was hugging me and everyone around her. Tears were streaming down her face. I didn't hear the final name read, but I could tell by the group's response that it was Jennifer. A couple boys next to her hoisted her onto their shoulders.

I wanted to slink away unnoticed, but Robyn had such a tight grip on my arm I couldn't squirm loose. I was happy for her, but what could I say? My mother reached over and hugged her. I tried to get past them.

"And the alternate for next year's squad . . ." Like a telegram from light-years away, I saw it coming. My name. Me. I heard it just before a dozen hands began thumping me on the back. Alternate. It wasn't a complete failure. I could still practice with the squad, even wear my uniform the day of a game. It meant Robyn and I would still be together.

I was smothered by bodies as happy/sad faces swarmed around us. Robyn still couldn't believe it. After everyone calmed down, Robyn and I slumped to the bleacher seats to recover.

"We did it," she said incredulously.

"How do you feel?" I asked. A foolish question. She exhaled and shook her head.

"Only one more thing would make this a perfect day," she said.

"What's that?"

"Weeble"—her eyes were serious—"my dad moved out today. They're going ahead with the divorce. Mom says they need 'space' to think things through."

"Why didn't you tell me earlier?"

"I didn't want to upset your concentration."

"*My* concentration?" I headlocked her with my arm and knuckled her head playfully. What a person, I thought. What a friend.

My mother had gone over to talk with Mr. Blair. I circled around behind them and snuck up to see if I could overhear what they were saying to each other. "Tomorrow at seven, then," my mother was agreeing.

So there was still hope for Mr. Blair, I realized. I wasn't going to get my hopes up, but if I had anything to say about the upcoming year, it would be the best yet. And tenth grade in the fall. My mother's arm had encircled my waist.

"You did it, Weeble!"